MAKE SIMPLICITY
YOUR SUPERPOWER!

MAKE SIMPLICITY YOUR SUPERPOWER!

COMMUNICATION HACKS
EVERY FINANCIAL ADVISOR
SHOULD KNOW

RICHARD DOBSON

Make Simplicity Your Superpower! by Richard Dobson
Public Domain. Reprint edition by Sound Wisdom, 2022

Published and Distributed by
SOUND WISDOM
PO Box 310
Shippensburg, PA 17257-0310
717-530-2122
info@soundwisdom.com
www.soundwisdom.com

ISBN 13: 978-1-64095-419-9
ISBN eBook: 978-1-64095-420-5

Note: This book is a product of its time and does not reflect the same views on race, gender, sexuality, ethnicity, and interpersonal relations as it would if it were written today.

For Worldwide Distribution, Printed in the U.S.A.
1 2 3 4 5 6 / 26 25 24 23 22

*Life is really simple, but we insist on
making it complicated.*

—CONFUCIUS

*You can't go back and change the beginning,
but you can start where you are
and change the ending.*

—C. S. LEWIS

CONTENTS

INTRODUCTION

*There are two mistakes one can make along the
road to truth...not going all the way, and not starting.*
—BUDDHA

A CRITICAL ASPECT OF winning and holding on to clients is making them feel comfortable, especially when we first meet them. One of the things I've noticed in my own career in the financial services industry, which now spans over four decades, is that it's all too easy to overwhelm prospective clients with technical information that is second nature to us as financial advisors, but unfamiliar and even a little intimidating to them. When people are intimidated, they don't feel comfortable. When they don't feel comfortable, they tend to disengage. When they disengage, we lose the opportunity to connect as people, to identify areas where we can add value to them and their families, and perhaps even to do business with them at all. When we try to explain too much, too soon, too fast, our prospective clients "check out." We may be tempted to drop miles and miles of hard-won technical expertise on prospective clients, for the simple reason that *we* know how important those long stretches of learning are to the establishment of a sound financial plan. But our clients and prospects don't share our perspective or our depth of knowledge. They need a more user-friendly approach, an approach that lays out essential concepts one at a time and in a manner that they can understand. For them, it's a matter of digesting one chunk of information at a time. That's what they're likely to be comfortable with. And consider: *We* acquired this knowledge one chunk at a time as well!

Sharing too much, too soon, with too much jargon, is a recipe for failure for a prospective client. My dad (who also chose a career as a financial planner) always reminded me of the importance of meeting people where they are and speaking at their level of understanding. He told me that "There is a lot to be said for brevity—just don't say too much!!" He was reminding me that making sure you are understandable is more important than making sure you show off all that you know. Simplicity in our communication with clients and prospective clients is not a flaw—it's a feature!

In later years, I came up with a phrase I could share with other financial professionals that would help them to remember this principle, now embodied in the system outlined in the book you are reading:

Make Simplicity Your Superpower!

INTRODUCTION

What follows is a process I've developed, using my own talking points, as well as the insights and illustrations of others, for bringing prospective clients "up to speed" on the foundational principles that support sound financial planning. All leverage the best practice—the superpower—of simplicity. This is a muscle that you can develop over time…if you choose. And I believe that if you do, it will deliver a competitive advantage that amounts to "super strength" in terms of your ability to connect on an emotional level with your clients.

What you are about to read is my effort to systematize something my father, like many successful financial professionals before him, knew and practiced: share a little bit of information, share it in a compelling way, and make sure it sticks before you move on. By the inch, it's a cinch!

I believe that we, as professionals, have an obligation to be clearly understood, and that this obligation is intimately connected to our obligation to act in the client's best interests. We can hardly be acting in the client's best interests if we don't determine what those interests are, and we can't find out what those interests are if the client can't understand us! We have an obligation to maintain a comprehensible dialogue with our clients at all times.

In order to communicate clearly, we must be disciplined enough to introduce one key concept at a time, and like a postage stamp, we must stick with it until it's delivered and we know that the other person has grasped the concept we are trying to get across.

We must avoid the temptation of acting as though we're talking to someone who has the same background we do. We should not try to eat the entire Thanksgiving dinner all at once; rather, it's best to go one bite at a time! We must meet people where they are, because if we don't, we can't help them. The more people we can communicate with in this way, the more people will want to do business with us. The more people who want to do business with us, the more people we can help. The more people we can help, the more successful we will become.

And really, what is the alternative? Confusing people? Alienating them? Giving them the impression that we are masters of some obscure discipline that they cannot ever hope to understand and demanding that they hand over the reins to us without asking any troublesome questions? That's not the kind of relationship I want with my client, and I assume it's not the kind of relationship you want with your clients, either.

Some years back, I received a referral from an associate of mine to a potential client who had what the associate described as a "complex history." Did he ever! This particular individual (I'll call him Cliff) had lost millions of dollars to the (once respected, now disgraced) financier Bernie Madoff. I am proud to be able to say that while a huge chunk of the money Cliff lost in that man's famous Ponzi scheme—the largest and most complex in recorded history—was impossible to reclaim, I did help my new client get back on his feet financially by means of a series of sober, direct, and honest conversations about what was happening in his life, financially and otherwise; what resources were still available to him; and what he wanted to see happen next. I mention this story not to impress you with any ability on my part to make the personal impact of massive financial fraud vanish without a trace, because I certainly was not able to do that. I tell you about Cliff to impress upon you what I learned from him about his experience with Madoff.

Bernie Madoff, it turns out, shunned one-on-one meetings and created a wizard-like aura, presenting himself to clients and prospective clients as some kind of mysterious higher presence, someone who knew things mere mortals could never know, who had connections mere mortals could only dream of, and who could deliver investment returns that most people thought were impossible. As it turned out, the supremacy he claimed over his clients was part of an elaborate, carefully curated, and ultimately doomed swindle. As I listened to Cliff speak of what his experiences with Madoff consisted of—Madoff's stark, ultra-modern, immaculate offices; his Wall Street pedigree; his casual references to supposedly high-level connections with regulators—I realized we were talking about someone who was an expert at impression management and posturing. It was all designed to deflect suspicion and questions. I found myself thinking of how much damage this man had done to the lives of his victims and how important it was for financial advisors to simplify their approach, to be sure they are understood and that they understand the client, and to make sure all the facts are on the table. This is part of our calling as professionals—and likely a regulatory obligation as well!

This man's modus operandi was to deflect all reasonable doubt and impress people, and thus to establish himself as their superior in every imaginable realm. Our ideal modus operandi is different: to connect with people as peers, as equals, and to make complex topics simple for them, one topic at a time. And this, I believe, is what all financial professionals should be striving to do.

This is, I believe, the most effective way of doing business: having simple, direct, and honest conversations with prospects and customers about what makes the most sense for them. We can explain important concepts to them, but we cannot understand those concepts for them. The ideas and examples you will find here have proven invaluable in my business in increasing the probability of being understood. I hope you will find them helpful in yours.

PART ONE

FOUNDATIONAL PRINCIPLES

CHAPTER ONE

STAY OUT OF COMPLEXITY MODE

If you can't explain it simply,
you don't understand it well enough.
—ALBERT EINSTEIN

Any darn fool can make something complex;
it takes a genius to make something simple.
—PETE SEEGER

MANY FINANCIAL ADVISORS, in my experience, suffer from a dark curse. I call it Complexity Mode, and I've seen its devastating impact, direct and indirect, up close and from a distance, virtually every working day of the four decades that I've been in this industry.

Complexity Mode is expensive. It costs us goodwill, engagement, referrals, positive word of mouth, and (last, but certainly not least) *business* from people who would be much better off working with us. Instead of working with us, they walk away shaking their heads.

It's quite likely you've fallen prey to Complexity Mode without even realizing it. Complexity Mode is so widespread among professionals that we actually have come to believe it is part of how we do business. And most of the time, we don't even know that the mode is affecting us or our practice—that's how accustomed we've grown to it. Just in case you've gotten used to it too, here is what it looks like in action. Take a look and decide for yourself if any of this sounds familiar.

- **We meet a prospective client for the first time.** We often meet people who have not investigated the core concepts of investments, insurance policies, tax planning, and retirement planning—unlike us, who not only understand those things but love to talk about them at length.

- **The opportunity arises for us to talk about whether it makes sense for us to work together.** This opportunity could come at the beginning of a scheduled face-to-face or voice-to-voice meeting during the working day, or it could come in a less structured social setting, such as a party or a networking venue.

- **We start explaining something.** Why? Because it's what we love to do. After all, we're trained professionals who know our own subject area backwards and forwards. Maybe we start explaining the details of a specific policy, investment, or retirement strategy. Maybe we start explaining about

XYZ Company, which we represent and which has such a bulletproof reputation and such a long and impressive history that we just can't help delivering a long monologue about it. Maybe we start explaining the foundational principles of an effective investment plan we worked on recently. Maybe we start explaining how we got into the business, where we went to school, how many different accreditations we have, and what those credentials mean. Maybe (and I have actually seen this happen) we start explaining about *all of the above* on the very first meeting—all before we've learned anything of consequence about the person to whom we're speaking.

- **What we're explaining doesn't stick.** It can't possibly make much sense to our prospective client. We've dumped too much information, too early. So, it goes right over their head, or worse yet, they now believe that they know all about you and/or your product or company and may feel there is no reason to schedule a meeting!

- **The prospective client starts to display a glazed, increasingly distracted expression about the eyes.** It's possible we didn't notice this, but it happened whether we noticed it or not. That facial expression is the legacy of Complexity Mode, and what we all need to do is learn to recognize it the moment it starts to appear. That faraway look marked the point where the person started to tune out of our conversation—because whether we realized it or not, we were subjecting them to a lesson they didn't ask for, in a language they didn't understand. And when that happens, *people tune out.* Note: You might have thought you were speaking English to your prospective client, when in fact you were speaking Finglish...Financial English. (Or, even worse, Meglish...Me-Based English, meaning English that is focused exclusively on the person who is doing the speaking.)

- **Politely or impolitely, slowly or in an accelerated way, directly by saying "Thanks but no thanks," or indirectly by asking for a little time to "think things over," this person calls the discussion, and the relationship, to a halt.** Even if it took us a while to stop talking (and it often does), communication ceased. And whether we see it or not, at some point the person shakes their head in confusion, dismay, or both—glad to escape, finally, from an uncomfortable situation.

That's what Complexity Mode looks like in action. How many prospects could you have turned into clients and helped their families achieve lifelong financial success, if not for this mode?

WHY WE DON'T "CLICK"

As a financial advisor, what you just read should be ringing a few bells. If you're honest with yourself, you'll admit that there have been plenty of times when things just didn't seem to "click" with a prospective client and that inability to "click" cost you a client or a referral.

My challenge to you now is a simple one: ask yourself *why* things didn't seem to click.

Here's one possible answer: As so many of us do, you fell prey to Complexity Mode. You did most of the talking, and the other person did hardly any talking at all. As a result, the person you were hoping to help achieve financial success ended up staring at you with a vacant, disengaged expression…and looking for the exit.

Why do we suffer from Complexity Mode? I believe there are three major reasons.

TECH TALK

The first reason is the **technical nature** of the solutions we provide and the services we offer.

Let's face it. There are a lot of moving parts to keep track of as a financial services professional and a lot of things that can go wrong if you don't keep track of all the different processes and checklists. It takes a special kind of person, a special kind of mind, to understand all those moving parts and make them work together effectively. Specifically, it takes someone who loves solving problems and who is careful not to skip any steps. Sometimes, we feel a professional obligation to identify *all* the potential problems and share *all* the steps necessary to prevent them, from our perspective—that of the expert. We forget that an equally important part of our job is to be translators, interpreters, and guides along the way for people who *aren't* experts and *can't* take in all the steps necessary to solve the problem. That is why the person is sitting in front of us!

WE LOVE OUR OWN VOICE

The second reason we fall prey to Complexity Mode is that **we genuinely love what we do and we love talking about it**.

There's nothing to be ashamed of in this. It's a good thing that we enjoy talking about the subjects we have a deep understanding of. We just need to recognize that not everyone else has the same level of knowledge and experience that we do. If a doctor walked up to you at a party and instantly started talking to you excitedly about the latest risk factors and treatment advances for the known subtypes of Hodgkin's lymphoma—nodular sclerosis, mixed cellularity, lymphocyte-depleted, and lymphocyte-rich—would you feel like an equal partner in the conversation? Or would you feel like you were in over your head? Most of us, even if we happen to suffer from the disease, would need some help grasping the doctor's points, no matter how much he loved his job.

CONNECTION ISSUES

Third and finally, **we haven't yet got expertise in developing an initial and ongoing sense of connection** with our prospective clients.

Many of us have not yet developed the same level of expertise in this critical area that we have developed in the area of solving someone's complex financial problems. To put it bluntly, we assume we're talking to fellow problem-solvers when we aren't—and unfortunately, that can turn off a large chunk of the population. We need to be able to appeal to a larger portion of the bell curve, very early in the relationship.

For us to be truly effective, we need to master a whole new skill that has little or nothing to do with solving a technical problem. It has everything to do with making sure that the essence of what we are doing, or planning to do, or recommending, actually *sticks in the other person's mind in a memorable and understandable way.* That skill is one that too many financial advisors have simply never been trained in: putting others at ease with who we are and what we do. It develops one of the most important things that we need to create and retain a lifetime client: trust.

For years now, I have been collecting and refining examples, insights, stories, and anecdotes that make it far easier for people to understand and remember exactly what financial advisors do, recommend, and warn against. Here is my promise to you: these strategies work.

The strategies I'll share in this book are proven, game-changing tools that promote conversation, thus helping our key points *stick* in a memorable, understandable way. These user-friendly metaphors will align us with those we want to help, make them more receptive to our messaging, and prevent that glazed expression that precedes their disengagement. These tools have the potential to transform our relationships with prospective clients—by making Complexity Mode a thing of the past.

But (isn't there always a "but" to deal with in life?) before we can even go there, we have to address a deeper problem, a challenge that can keep even the very best example or metaphor from having its intended effect: our own inability to create a sense of personal connection between us and the people with whom we interact. If we don't deal with that problem first, there's no point in trying to utilize any of the other concepts I'll be sharing in this book.

So, with all of that in mind, please consider accepting my personal invitation to make this book your coach. Some of these ideas will become your favorites and can be jogged to memory by a client's comment or remark.

Please consider working with me to remove Complexity Mode from *all* your future interactions with clients and prospective clients.

Let's get started!

CHAPTER TWO

HOW TO BUILD RAPPORT

Complexity is perplexing...
unless you know how to see.
—THOMAS VATO

Take the first step in faith.
You don't have to see the whole staircase,
just take the first step.
—MARTIN LUTHER KING, JR.

IT'S TIME TO TAKE a closer look at the implications of Complexity Mode, the syndrome that allows financial professionals to lapse into an "Analysis Mindset" at the very beginning of the relationship with their prospective client.

Financial advisors face a difficult challenge. It is this: we are problem-solvers. That's what we do. That's how we define ourselves. We are the people who spot inconsistencies. We are the ones who identify important steps that may have been overlooked along the way. We are the ones who spot potentially catastrophic errors that other people—people who aren't financial professionals—might never have known existed. We spot and fix problems. We figure out solutions. The difficulty is that our skill at problem-solving is sometimes the very thing that pushes prospective clients away from us.

Why is that? Glad you asked!

When someone first reaches out to us, first meets with us face to face or discusses the possibility of working with us, we may feel slightly uncomfortable. We may not be sure how to take this conversation and prospect and turn them into a new client for our practice. So, what do we do instinctively? Very often, when we're placed in a stressful situation (like converting a stranger into a client), we fall back on that which is most familiar to us, most comfortable to us, what we're most used to doing.

What's most familiar and comfortable to us? The act of solving problems, of course. So, if the person we're talking to happens to mention that they have a tax issue, we're likely to jump right into the fray and start trying to solve that problem immediately…thinking that proving our expertise is the very best way to convince the prospect that we are the advisor for them. So, we start analyzing—and we start talking. We move into the Analysis Mindset.

We start lecturing. We start identifying all the possible things that could have gone wrong in the past and might be going wrong now or in the future, which connect to that person's tax issue.

And in doing so, we may turn the other person off.

What the person is looking for is *emotional comfort within the relationship*—a sense that it's safe to talk to us, interact with us, and work with us; a sense that we are approachable and trustworthy. And unfortunately, going into the Analysis Mindset often has exactly the opposite effect. It can make the person we're talking to feel lectured at, overwhelmed, and talked down to…even though that wasn't our intent at all. Can you guess what people who are feeling lectured at, over-whelmed, and talked down to do when they find themselves trapped in a social situation?

They find a reason to leave. They may leave by saying that they're glad they met us. They may leave by saying that they will be in touch. They may even leave by saying that they're looking forward to talking to us again. But they don't mean any of those things. What they really mean is, "I'm saying these words to make it less awkward for me to terminate this conversation and never follow through with connecting with you."

What we shared with them about tax planning (or any other topic) didn't stick. It didn't even register. It just created a bubble of discomfort. And a lost business opportunity.

That's Complexity Mode in action. And understanding this mode represents our first and most important challenge as financial professionals. We need to accept that approaching a client relationship with an Analysis Mindset simply doesn't work. It doesn't establish our credibility. It doesn't give the person we're talking to deeper confidence in our ability to solve problems. All it does is make people uncomfortable and encourage them to find a reason to leave and never come back.

Each of the chapters in the main section of this book contains a single important takeaway, a best practice you can adopt immediately to improve the quality of your conversations, and your relationships, with clients and prospective clients.

KEY TAKEAWAY

The aim in any early discussion with a prospective client isn't to solve a problem, prove a point, or show how smart you are...it's to connect on an emotional level that the other person will remember. And YOU will remember also!

People will remember how you made them feel for far longer than they remember what you said. If you don't make them feel good about working with you, NOTHING WILL STICK!

In your initial interaction with a possible (or current) client, your job is simply to stay out of the Analysis Mindset.

What should you do instead? *Connect on a personal level with this individual.* Establish commonality. Shake hands warmly. Make unthreatening eye contact as you do so. Ask questions about the other person that show that you have a genuine interest in his or her world. Start or support a conversation that *isn't* about your area of expertise. Ask more questions!

Once you have done that, look for clear signs of comfort, relaxation, and engagement *before* you address any financial question or issue—and stay out of the Analysis Mindset *until* you see those signs. They include smiling, laughter, relaxed body language, and the expressed desire (on the prospective client's part) to "get down to business." Let *them* make that transition! Follow their lead.

If you stay out of the Analysis Mindset and establish a genuine rapport with the other person, you will have overcome the first half of Complexity Mode. The second half of that mode is just as dangerous. We'll take a closer look at it in the next chapter.

CHAPTER THREE

THE ART OF SETTING EXPECTATIONS

We are drowning in information
but starved for knowledge.
—JOHN NAISBITT

Information is only useful when
it can be understood.
—MURIEL COOPER

THE SECOND HALF OF Complexity Mode is just as serious as failing to establish rapport. It's setting the wrong expectation for the discussion—and the relationship as a whole.

We have to remember: Our goal for our meeting with the prospect isn't to turn them into experts. It isn't to impart academic knowledge. It isn't to make them employees of our practice. It's to *identify their needs and then demonstrate, in a compelling way, that they can count on us to address those needs and to be understood.*

Anything else is just noise. We want them to *rely* on us, the experts. That means we need to be willing to set aside technical or academic knowledge and emphasize *human* knowledge. That's what all the tools I'll be sharing with you in the chapters that follow are designed to do: move away from the technical or academic knowledge of financial decisions (which is all about numbers) and focus consistently on human knowledge (which is all about emotions).

The second half of Complexity Mode can cause the prospective client to think that we are all about the numbers and have no interest in the emotions. That's a big mistake and a major competitive vulnerability.

You may have seen the State Farm Insurance commercial in which a robot is trying to hold up one end of a conversation with real, live human beings. The results, as you might expect, are not ideal. That's what we're trying to avoid—the perception that we don't want and can't sustain a human-to-human connection with the other person, that we are simply a mechanical presence. We need to be able to focus on the emotions, not just the numbers. Remember: this issue will always resonate with clients. You can come off as a robot if you're not careful. You must focus on the emotions first.

To illustrate exactly what I mean by "focusing on the emotions," consider the following scenario. You're meeting for the first time with a prospective client. You've moved past the phase of establishing a comfortable conversation and good one-on-one chemistry with this prospective client—we'll call him Bill—and you start going over his account statements. Before you can glean any meaningful information, however, Bill says to you, "There was a huge drop in the market this quarter, and my equity holdings have lost 15 percent, which is a lot. That's pretty scary. I think maybe it's time to get out while the getting is good."

How would you respond?

A lot of financial advisors—even after having established a good initial person-to-person bond with Bill—would go into the Lecture Mindset, in support of the principle of taking a long-term perspective on such decisions. As it turns out, the Lecture Mindset is just as dangerous as the Analysis Mindset, and perhaps even more so. It's the financial advisor equivalent of a doctor with a terrible bedside manner.

In the Lecture Mindset, you set out to demonstrate all the data points that prove beyond a shadow of a doubt that *Bill is wrong and you are right*. So, you start pulling out charts that demonstrate the market history. You start talking about long-term trends and comparing them to short-term trends. And you basically start giving a seminar on the statistical justification for taking a long-term view of investment analysis.

All of which is technically correct, but dead wrong from the human point of view.

Now suppose you were to take a different approach with Bill. Suppose you were to begin your reply by *acknowledging the emotions he is feeling at the moment.* In other words, before you even address the question of what should or shouldn't be done next, suppose you were to say something like this to Bill:

"I know what you mean about how it's feeling scary out there. The stock market has been on a real roller-coaster ride lately, hasn't it?"

And suppose you were to *stop talking* at that point—so as to allow Bill to further express his feelings about the last quarter.

Sometimes people need to vent. Sometimes they need to express their feelings. Sometimes they need to process what they've been going through. That's true of what happens in their personal lives, it's true of what happens to them at work, and it's definitely true of what happens to their money!

So, we need to take that into account. We need to express *empathy*—which is the ability to feel the same emotion your client is feeling and openly identify with it—before we even talk about the specific problem he or she has raised.

Empathy is a critical communication skill, one that the most successful financial advisors learn to master. It is the opposite of the Lecture Mindset, because where the Lecture Mindset tells the other person to sit still, listen carefully, and perhaps take notes, the Empathy Mindset lets the other person know that it's okay to vent and to share how he or she feels about what's happened. Notice that empathy is very different from *sympathy*. Sympathy says, "Your assessment of the situation is correct, and I agree with your emotional response to it." Empathy just says, "I know what it's like to feel that way, and I can identify with that feeling."

PARTICIPANT-CENTERED LEARNING

Once you have an understanding of how the other person feels and you have expressed empathy for his or her emotional state, you can move on to asking a question, one that gets the other person involved in an ongoing dialogue with some emotional depth. This is *participant-centered* learning. It's the most effective learning model there is—learning that's based on authentic back-and-forth engagement between two human beings.

This kind of learning is, I believe, the very best, and probably the most effective, way of teaching. I prefer to call this kind of teaching by the name by which it has become popular in recent years—participant-centered learning—but I recognize it goes by many names.

KEY TAKEAWAY

Participant-centered learning is based on the premise that getting learners *actively engaged* is the most effective way to get them to retain and actually *use* the learning content. This type of learning is devoted to the idea of getting the learner to *do* something—not just sit there passively and listen to us talk!

It's estimated that we retain only 10 percent of what we *read;* 20 percent of what we *hear* when listening to a talk or lecture; 50

percent of what we *see and hear* by (for instance) attending an exhibition, watching a demonstration, or watching a video; 70 percent of what we *say* out loud; and a staggering 90 percent of what we *do!* Is it any wonder that engaged participants in a conversation about financial strategies—people who take part in a real discussion and encounter visual and physical learning aids—put more of what they learn into action than people who sit passively and listen? Combine the learning modes, and the retention rates go sky-high!

Participant-centered learning is, therefore, *interactive* learning with multiple points of sensory input. It's learning that meets the needs of its audience. It's learning that is engaging and relevant to the audience's life situation. It's learning that puts the audience first by providing relevant content, emphasizing the quality of content over the quantity of content, and giving the audience time and space to process what they've learned. Participant-centered learning is the path toward, not just the accumulation of facts, but the accumulation of *wisdom.*

Participant-centered learning actually goes all the way back to Socrates! What else would you call the classic teaching method known as Socratic questioning? Someone has a question. You draw that person out and respond with a question of your own. That's engagement!

So, once Bill has expressed his feelings, and not before, we can *concisely and empathetically* share another take on the situation he's facing. I'll be sharing lots of these examples with you in the pages that follow, but for now, consider the possibilities that remain open in the following dialogue, which is the polar opposite of the Lecture Mindset.

Bill: There was a huge drop in the market this week, and my equity holdings have lost 15 percent, which is a lot. That's pretty scary. I think maybe it's time to get out while the getting is good.

You: I know what you mean about it feeling scary out there. The stock market has been on a real roller-coaster ride this week, hasn't it?

Bill: It certainly has. It seemed like my wife was glued to the TV all week, watching the Dow Jones numbers go down. She kept talking about how, by doing nothing, we were destroying our daughter's college fund.

You: A stock market slide can be very tough to watch. I know. Can I ask how old your daughter is?

Bill: She's seven.

You: Okay. Well, Bill, we've got a lot to go over today, and I certainly understand your concern and your wife's concern about your daughter's college fund. But can I share something I've learned over the years about market downturns?

Bill: Sure.

You: Since we've got at least a decade before your daughter is going to need those funds for college, I want to suggest we step back a little bit and look at the history before we make any decisions today. A market downturn is a bit like driving on a dark road late at night. It definitely can feel scary, because you don't know what turns are coming up or how sharp they're going to be. But you know what? If you flip on the high beams, you can get a much better look at where the road is going, and it's a lot less scary to drive that road. Can I share some thoughts with you about how we might flip on the high beams and get a look at the longer term?

Bill: Yeah, that sounds like a good idea. Go ahead.

Notice that validating Bill's emotion has gotten him to a place where his mind is a little bit more open to the possibility of following your lead. Notice, too, that what has followed that emotional validation is not a lecture, but a *conversation* that involves Bill and seeks his input and participation. The only way to move the conversation forward—the only way to move the *relationship* forward—is to engage Bill as a peer, as someone with insights and experiences that deserve to be considered within the context of your conversation.

It's very similar to the situation that exists between a good doctor and a patient. Only the doctor has medical training—but only the patient has the direct experience of what's going on with his or her body. There needs to be an effective two-way exchange of information between peers. If that is lacking, there's going to be a communication breakdown somewhere along the line!

Complexity Mode kills conversations. Empathy opens them up and then sets the stage for a discussion that is all about Bill and his issues. Again, that's participant-centered learning, and we must constantly remind ourselves that it's the single most effective learning model for adults. Participant-centered learning is what this book is all about.

Each tool shared in this book is designed to put the focus of the conversation on a specific kind of solution *you* can provide.

Notice that your personal goal is to be known for the problems you solve, not the products you sell. Consider that there are hundreds of thousands of power drills out there, but in the end, people are not so much concerned with the type of power drill they use as they are with making the hole that they are using the power drill to create, in an efficient manner. In your case, the solution you are providing is usually a sound, realistic retirement plan, one that avoids unnecessary risk and makes intelligent choices that minimize the investor's tax exposure. Consider that to be the "hole" that your prospective client is interested in drilling. Resist the temptation to start talking in depth about the capacity of the drill! (It's what the product *does* that counts. That is where the excitement is.)

PART TWO

THE COMMUNICATION HACKS

CHAPTER FOUR

IN THE BEGINNING...

The beginning is the most
important part of the work.

—PLATO

Great things are done by a series
of small things brought together.

—VINCENT VAN GOGH

KEY TAKEAWAY

In this section of the book, you will learn to use the resources I call FINANCIAL ADVISOR'S COMMUNICATION HACKS.

YOU CAN THINK OF the communication hacks that appear in this section of the book as being analogous to Post-it® notes. Think for a moment about why those are so popular. If you write a few words on a standard piece of paper and then try to attach it to a wall as is, it will fall to the floor. If you write the same words on a sticky note, peel it off the deck, and apply it to the wall...presto! It stays there for as long as you need it!

The stories, illustrations, and examples I'll be sharing with you in the chapters that follow work in exactly the same way. Each one takes a concept or insight that makes intuitive sense to us, as financial professionals—but that is unlikely to "stick" when presented to someone without a financial background. By supplementing that concept or insight with the right context, presentation, or "sizzle," however, we can make sure the idea gets across in a memorable way and stays in the person's "top-of-mind" awareness for as long as he or she needs it. That's the best communication hack there is.

Your first communication hack, which I encourage you to familiarize yourself with and then use comfortably and informally in a participant-centered learning conversation (not as a "lecture topic"), dramatizes the concept that human beings have a natural inclination to avoid risk and loss...and the related concept that people expect their monetary investments to appreciate over time.

Ready? Here we go.

A LONG, LONG TIME AGO...

Eleven thousand five hundred years ago, in what is now known as the Jordan Valley, our Neolithic ancestors designed, built, and maintained hut-like structures that archaeologists and other scientists have confirmed were used for a very specific purpose: keeping food safe. The huts had elevated floors; the people who built them sealed them in completely with mud so that rodents and other vermin couldn't get in. It was apparent to scientists that this work was done with great care.

Understand: This happened a long, long time ago.

These huts were built in the period before the rise of domestic agriculture; we're talking about the period after the early Stone Age but before the Bronze Age. At this stage in human history, there were no cities (as we would understand the word "city") and there were no advanced civilizations. Domestication of animals like dogs had only just begun. We have no evidence that writing had been developed yet during this period. The first currency wouldn't show up for over ten thousand years.

But there were these huts, constructed for the specific purpose of keeping insects, animals, and (presumably) unauthorized human beings from stealing or spoiling the food supply. In fact, even though these huts have been connected to a certain historical period, it's likely that the specific motivation for creating them predates the Neolithic era by some time. I believe this motivation has been with us as human beings from the very beginning, from the earliest days of humanity's time on earth.

Now…why do I mention all this?

To prove this point: The instinct to protect assets, to identify potential risks to those assets, and to take action to minimize those risks, is primal. It's hardwired into the human species.

This instinct is part of who we are. We've been following it for a very, very, very long time. Longer than we've been writing. Longer than we've been farming. Longer than we've been building cities. This instinct to protect our most critical assets, to shield them from risks, is a fundamental component of who we are as human beings. It's as central to our identity as the will to survive and protect our loved ones—and indeed, it's a core component of those two goals.

Some unknown number of millennia ago, tribes and clans recognized that there was a risk of losing a precious asset: food—and they set up a strategic plan to protect that asset.

The assets we aim to protect today may look a little different, but the instinct that drives us to set up a plan to protect them is exactly the same. Eventually, that instinct led us to develop the idea of agriculture, so we could raise, harvest, and secure food with greater predictability and control.

Now, here's an interesting bit of perspective for you. We still have a plan for protecting food from outside threats. One of the modern expressions of that plan takes the form of a structure we call a grain elevator. Sometimes referred to as "temples of the prairie," many are over ninety feet tall—they dwarf the huts the archaeologists found in the Jordan Valley, and they're much better designed. They're far more effective at keeping out rodents and other vermin. But you know what? They still aren't anywhere close to perfect. Even with all our new technology and advances in the storage and handling of food, we ultimately lose 20 percent or more of the crops we harvest. (One can only imagine what the spoilage rate was for those ancient huts. I suppose it all depended on how long you expected to leave the food in the hut!) The thing to bear in mind is, even today, in the twenty-first century, we accept a loss to our assets when the asset is food.

But we *don't* accept a slow, gradual decline in the *money* assets we set out to protect. We expect them to grow over time!

KEY TAKEAWAY

We don't want our money to just sit there. We expect it to increase in value. And fortunately—miraculously—that expectation has proved to be realistic...when the right plan is in place.

So, this is one of the ways human society has definitely moved forward since the Neolithic era. No one who stored food in that hut 11,500 years ago expected there to be *more* edible food in it than he or she placed in the hut in the first place. Yet today, we not only have reliable, repeatable strategies for protecting our most important assets, we actually have any number of strategies that cause those assets to *increase* over time!

The question is, how do you identify what those strategies are? How do you communicate them? And how do you implement them?

CHAPTER FIVE

TWO WAYS TO MAKE MONEY

*An investment in knowledge
pays the best interest.*
—BENJAMIN FRANKLIN

Money often costs too much.
—RALPH WALDO EMERSON

THE NEXT COMMUNICATION HACK dramatizes the concept that human labor is one of two critical resources at our disposal. The other is our investments, which can work when we don't (or can't).

As with all the communication hacks you will find in this book, I strongly encourage you to familiarize yourself with this one ahead of time and then use it comfortably and informally in casual back-and-forth conversation…not as a "lecture topic." Notice that this communication hack naturally follows the IN THE BEGINNING communication hack (in chapter 4) and may fit in well after that conversation.

HOW TO MAKE MONEY

The decision that our ancient ancestors made to create structures capable of preserving and protecting food is worth thinking about closely. Why? Because the act of protecting a resource like food represents a pivot point in human civilization. At some point, many centuries ago, we humans began to think about storing our excess resources so that we would be able to handle the family's or the tribe's future needs…instead of just handing out all those resources the minute they became available. In a word, we began *saving*.

As we've seen, when we save food, that's a fixed resource. We don't expect it to grow over time once we store it. But other resources, like money, are different. We *can* expect certain resources to appreciate in value over time if we manage them properly. And here's why that's so important. *Fortunately for us all, human society eventually reached a point where the tribe or the family moved beyond just having enough to get by for the day.*

We moved beyond the short-term, immediate-gratification hunter-gatherer mode, and we started to plan a different kind of society, one where we could think in the longer term and use our resources in a way that supports us and the people who are close to us, not just today, but far into the future. That's what a hut designed to store excess food does, and that's what a financial system does too. The financial system may be based on beads, on coins, on banknotes, on bitcoin, or encoded in electronic chips. But its purpose is to help us manage our resources, and specifically our excess resources, intelligently over time.

Imagine the change. We weren't constantly out seeking food; we had a storehouse that freed up our time to focus on other things. It seems simple now, but it must have been a powerful and profound change when it first happened. And it began a progression that became vitally important to our species. We were now planning for tomorrow—and, by extension, for times beyond tomorrow when we might not have been able to secure resources as easily as we could today. This was a tremendous breakthrough. We began planning ahead to accommodate challenges we couldn't yet identify but that we knew we would someday face. Perhaps storage led our Neolithic ancestors to start thinking of cultivation, which would lead eventually to thoughts of developing a system of intentional farming—an even longer-term planning exercise, requiring much greater foresight.

Think of the basic unit of any human society: the family. Why is it there? What does it do? It supports and protects the various family members. The parents of an infant know that there will be challenges that threaten the safety and even the life of their child—falling from a height, say, or eating something dangerous—and they plan ahead to minimize the possible negative impacts of those challenges. A year goes by, and the likely challenges have shifted, but the parents' vigilance hasn't. They're still responsible for looking out for the child. A decade passes. The likely dangers have shifted again, but the parents still feel the personal responsibility to look after the child. Now five decades pass...and the child is pondering the dangers that may confront the parent. This is what a family does. It uses our human resources—our intelligence, our strength, our experience from past situations—to protect those who are accepted as members of the family from these outside threats.

The emergence of a financial system, of currency, and of mechanisms for saving money presented another, equally powerful method for protecting ourselves and our loved ones from potential threats. We can store up cash. And in so doing, we can shield ourselves and our loved ones from dangers and threats that we may not be able to address effectively on a personal level. We may be too old or too inexperienced, for instance, to feel comfortable taking on the responsibility of personally building a house for a grandchild...but we can save up the cash necessary to pay someone else to do that when the time comes.

So, there came a point when humans developed this fascinating new innovation called money. At least initially, it's a good bet that they did so as an ingenious strategy for meeting important family obligations. There are a lot of other things we can do with money, of course, but from the point of view of our own cultural evolution, it seems likely that it emerged first and foremost as a means of shielding ourselves and those close to us from danger. That's a major leap forward in our social development.

Here's the interesting thing about money, something we already discovered in the first communication hack: if you manage it properly, it can actually increase in value over time. The realization of that fact surely marks another major leap forward in our social development. We don't know when this particular breakthrough occurred, but we can be sure that when it did, it changed everything! Unlike human labor performed right now, in real time, *money is an asset that can be stored and can increase in value while we aren't using it.*

This means that if we have excess financial resources now, we can set them aside so that they can grow and we can have access to an even *greater* excess when we need it—which may be at a time when we're not able, or inclined, to do the equivalent work ourselves in person. This leads us to another key point: *money is important to our future.* In fact, it's the means whereby we plan and shape that future.

KEY TAKEAWAY

There are really only two ways to make money— *by putting a person to work or by putting the money to work.*

Putting ourselves to work is fine in theory…but it shouldn't be the only tool in our toolbox. Why not? Because our own capacity for labor will deplete over time. Our physical strength, our intelligence, our willingness to work, our ability to manipulate critical resources like wood and stone—all of these things will diminish with time. It's just the nature of the human experience. People simply aren't as capable when it comes to doing manual labor, or any other type of labor, at age ninety-five as they are at age twenty-five. That's the reality we face.

Money, however, is another matter. Putting our money to work intelligently *can* generate richer rewards tomorrow than it does today, and a financial asset wisely invested *is* capable of outperforming itself as time passes.

This is why we generally want to build both halves of the equation—putting ourselves to work *and* putting our money to work, by saving it and investing it wisely—into a sound financial plan.

A reminder: Your client—the person who's sitting across from you—already has this primal, innate knowledge that it is important to plan ahead. It's already there. For most clients, all you have to do is tap into it.

CHAPTER SIX

TWO KINDS OF INVESTMENTS

*Money is only a tool. It will take you
wherever you wish, but it will not
replace you as the driver.*

—AYN RAND

*If we command our wealth,
we shall be rich and free.
If our wealth commands us,
we are poor indeed.*

—EDMUND BURKE

THE NEXT COMMUNICATION HACK should be used only *after* TWO WAYS TO MAKE MONEY. This communication hack helps you land the point that despite the seemingly infinite range of investment possibilities, all of our investments really break down into two basic categories: you can loan or you can own.

As with all the communication hacks, I encourage you to familiarize yourself with and then use this one comfortably and informally in casual conversation…not as a "lecture topic."

Ready? Here we go.

TWO KINDS OF VEHICLES

The example we just learned about—the food stored by our ancient ancestors—dealt with a tangible, easy-to-understand type of asset: a specific *possession*; in this case, food. A possession, of course, is something you own, something specific that has value that belongs only to you. You can give it away or sell it or use it or ignore it as you see fit. So, let's say you raised a hundred bushels of potatoes, and then you stored them in a safe place, following the example of our ancient ancestors. Those potatoes would be your *possessions*. You could use them to feed your family, or plant new potato crops with them, or sell them to your neighbors, or even give them away. That's in the nature of possessions: you own them, and you get to say what happens with them. If the market price of potatoes rises, your potato equity goes up. If the price of potatoes falls, your potato equity goes down.

Another word for the possessions you might own—meaning your safely stored potatoes and anything else that you rightfully claim ownership of—is *equity*. When we say that you have built up *equity* in your home, we are talking about that portion of the home that you can claim as value *owned by you*, once you set aside any amounts owned by someone else (like the unpaid mortgage amount you still owe the lender). That equity is something you own. It's under your control. You and you alone get to decide what you want to do with it. If your home's market value goes up, the equity in your home goes up. If the market value of your home goes down, your equity goes down.

Equity, then, is one kind of investment we can choose to make with the resources at our disposal. We can invest in something that we *own*.

Back in the twelfth century, the city fathers of Venice, Italy, came up with another kind of investment. Realizing that they needed money for things like defending the city against invasion and building new bridges, they decided to create a brand-new kind of financial instrument: the bond.

What did bonds do? Simple: Bonds allowed the government to *borrow money* from people who chose to purchase them. The word *bond* means simply "promise." The city of Venice came up with the brilliant idea of writing up a document *promising* to repay the amount someone agreed to loan the city government, *plus a premium*—the agreed-upon interest accrued—in exchange for those people letting the city borrow the funds from them for a specified period of time.

The idea worked. People trusted the city government to pay back the money loaned. The city made good on its promises and repaid the loans, plus the agreed-upon interest. And a new type of investment was born—the bond, also known as a debt instrument.

These two simple examples—the potatoes in the storage shed and the document promising to repay the money loaned to the city of Venice—described the entire universe of investment possibilities. Our investments could be *equities,* meaning something that we own, either in whole or in part, which may go up or down in value; or our investments could be *debt instruments*, meaning loans that come in disguise, such as bank savings accounts, certificates of deposit, fixed annuity programs, and of course corporate, municipal, and utility bonds. In each of these cases, we choose to loan someone money in exchange for a guaranteed return. We may not think of these as loans, but that's what they are.

(Bonds guarantee dividends for the length of the bond and principal at maturity; in the interim, the principal or "market" value can fluctuate.)

KEY TAKEAWAY

For centuries, owning or loaning was the whole range of investment possibilities, broken down to their simplest levels. Humanity hadn't come up with any other kind of investment. No matter how complex an investment may have seemed, it could be assigned to one of those two categories. It was either something we owned (equity) or a loan we made to someone in anticipation of a premium (a debt instrument).

A sidenote is in order here. In the late twentieth century, humans finally came up with what might be considered a third type of investment, a hybrid category that falls in between debt and equity. These plans that fall "in between" owning and loaning are called "fixed indexed annuities." As the name suggests, they use an index of equities—say, the Standard and Poor's 500—in a consistent formula that determines what rate will be credited to the investor based on a given stock index's value, year by year. So instead of receiving a fixed interest-rate payment, the investor receives a payment based on a formula that includes the annual growth of the equity index in the equation. Although there are many variations, these hybrid investments can produce the expected results for clients, with the potential to create safe returns without the risk of a direct market investment. If equity is what you own and debt is something that you loan out, we can categorize this hybrid category as *Loanership*. It combines parts of both worlds. These plans are fixed annuities with a potentially higher return than a non-indexed fixed annuity.

One more brief note: You will occasionally hear it said of fixed index annuities that "you can own an index with zero market risk." This is not accurate and not appropriate to say to clients or prospective clients, because the client will never actually *own* the index; therefore, their money is not in equities, nor is it exposed to that risk. Rather, it is in a fixed annuity, which is also why any dividends are excluded as well.

CHAPTER SEVEN

NO LOAD OR NO HELP?

If you don't know where you are going...
you might not get there.

—YOGI BERRA

Believe passionately in what you do,
and never knowingly compromise your standards
and values. Act like a true professional, aiming for
true excellence, and the money will follow.

—DAVID MAISTER

THIS COMMUNICATION HACK is helpful for those situations where a prospective client starts talking excitedly to you about a particular investment he or she wants to make, based on the fact that the investment is a so-called "no-load" fund.

It's quite common for a client to walk in the door with his or her mind set on a specific type of investment that they have seen promoted or advertised somewhere. In this case, the person may say, "I want to put all my money in XYZ Fund because it's a no-load fund."

Of course, you know and I know that the fact that there is no load doesn't mean that there's no cost. This fund will still charge fees—they just won't charge for the sale at the time that the sale is made. Rather than going into the minutiae of how the charges work and whether paying a commission is a good idea, however, I have found it helpful to relate this classic analogy from Nick Murray.

Imagine that you're going on your annual visit to the doctor. And imagine, too, that the doctor sits you down and says, "Guess what? I've scheduled you for open-heart surgery. You go under the knife for heart surgery first thing tomorrow morning."

At that point, if you are a savvy patient, you will be well within your rights to ask, "Gee, doc, do I need heart surgery? You haven't even examined me yet!"

Suppose the doctor were to reply, "Well, no, you don't actually need open-heart surgery, but the best part about it is that we're not going to charge you for it."

That heart surgeon might as well be known as the no-load cardiologist. He's not going to charge you a fee for the operation;

but whether or not he does, he is skipping an important step. He's not figuring out whether the procedure is even necessary.

This is a very potent analogy because it isolates the fact that many people who are attracted to no-load funds are skipping the step of getting some guidance, advice, up-front examination, and experience to help them in their decision-making. They mistakenly base their decision solely on price.

KEY TAKEAWAY

An investor is completely on his or her own when it comes to no-load funds.

That investor is going to talk to a different person every single time he or she picks up the phone. That investor may get guidance…but not advice. You wouldn't expect legal advice from someone who isn't an attorney. By the same token, people who aren't qualified are prohibited from making recommendations about what you should buy, sell, or hold. And typically, sound financial advice from someone who knows your situation intimately is what is most sorely needed. You need a holistic overview—not just a sense of what everyone else is doing, but what is right for you, based on your unique history.

In the world of medicine, you expect a personalized diagnosis from your doctor; in the world of finance, you should expect a personalized diagnosis from a financial services professional. The difference between what a qualified professional delivers and what an amateur delivers can be immense—and it can definitely have an impact on the quality of your life. Long-term data shows us that no-load investors leave the market in droves during downturns, while advisor clients are far less likely to behave this way. In short, no-load investors tend to react while advisor-led clients tend to form responses. Just like in the medical sense, we should respond, not react, to situations.

Technically, there is a lower up-front cost to no-load funds, yes, but that cost is only a consideration in the absence of value. Could someone get to work by driving a beat-up 1972 Volkswagen Beetle? Sure. Is doing so less expensive than getting to work by driving a new Lexus? Of course. But some people make the choice to arrive with a little more dependability and a little more style…and they make that extra investment because they see additional value in the choice to drive a Lexus.

It's the same way with investment advice. There is definitely value there—and it is your job as a financial services professional to identify your value and to stand behind it. One of the ways I like to do that is to say, at some point during the initial discussion with a prospective client, "In addition to a great plan and great products—you also get me!" From one perspective, it's humorous…but from another perspective, it really is about the value we deliver and our own willingness to take a stand for it.

Consider saying something like the following to your client. Let's say you had planned for years to take a trip to the Amazon. Let's say you finally arranged that trip, and now you have landed in Brazil with no knowledge of the people, the terrain, or the wildlife. How comfortable would you be exploring the depths of the rainforest without a qualified guide to help you experience all the natural beauty—and keep you out of harm's way? Sure, you could buy a book and do your best to guide yourself. But would that really be the wisest and safest course of action? In order to make the odds of a successful and safe trip as high as possible, you want a seasoned, knowledgeable, and experienced guide by your side. It's just the same as the financial journey you are making. Because there are real dangers, in addition to real opportunities, you need to choose someone you can trust, someone who knows the terrain and how to avoid all the hazards, to help you get around. Remember my client, Cliff? He now knows the importance of selecting the right guide.

By the way, my father, my brother, and I did make such a trip to the Amazon in 2009, and we did have our experienced guide,

Brahma, by our side the entire time. Were we ever glad that we did! Manaus, Brazil, located in the heart of the Amazon, has a population of over two million, and there were plenty of potential dangers. Brahma would always run interference for us, and any hazards were successfully avoided. A seasoned guide, a trusted professional who knows how to keep people out of trouble—that's the role you were trained for and that your clients expect at a minimum. No-load investors are notorious for misinterpreting a temporary decline as a permanent loss and then taking action to make it so. A good advisor is what stands in the way of this inappropriate action. The best advisors use their knowledge, experience, and long-term outlook to keep clients from stumbling when outlooks are darkest. Keep them on the right path and steer them away from danger. Be your client's Brahma.

BRAHMA

Your Success in Brazil

Ph: (55-92) 9994-2779
Fx: (55-92) 3664-0623

E-mail: brahma@interlins.com.br

CHAPTER EIGHT

FIRE AND ICE

I will tell you the secret to getting rich on Wall Street.
You try to be greedy when others are fearful.
And you try to be fearful when others are greedy.
—WARREN BUFFETT

Everybody wants to go to heaven, but nobody wants to die.
—LORETTA LYNN

USE THIS COMMUNICATION HACK to set realistic expectations about returns and time frames…and to help clients keep fluctuations in the equity markets in perspective.

Both investors and financial professionals suffer from a common problem: short-term perspective. They tend to focus on what's going on over a time span of three to six months, as opposed to the longer time frame in which investment activity really needs to be evaluated—the span of decades that's most relevant to the human life span. Here's how that sometimes plays out: Bob Investor goes to a party, and he hears a friend of a friend say something like, "I made such-and-such an investment, and it delivered a 28 percent return!" So, the next time Bob sits down with his financial advisor, he wants to hear all about "creative" investments that deliver a 28 percent return.

What's missing from that discussion?

A sense of perspective—and specifically a clear sense of the span of time over which a given investment is being measured. Let's set aside the reality that the investment figures that people throw around at parties tend to get more dramatic, and further removed from reality, the more often they are repeated. Let's assume that 28 percent is actually how a given investment performed. The big question here is, over what length of time?

You know and I know that numbers like that are highly unlikely over time spans of five, ten, or twenty years. But individual investors don't necessarily know that. And it's our job to help them figure it out...and to set clear, realistic expectations about returns and time frames. Here's one great way to do that. It's a communication hack you can use to begin a conversation about setting accurate expectations when it comes to investment returns.

You and I (I tell investors) don't want to invest in the short term. I can't help you set up a plan that's going to make you rich in six months, and it wouldn't be fair (or legal) of me to claim that I could. What you and I are out to do is make good investment choices over the longer term. And to do that, we need to take a good, long look at how different types of investments have performed over much longer periods of time. The regulators have a saying: "Past performance is no guarantee of future results." That's true, and it's definitely worth bearing in mind. But at the same time, since we know we can't predict the future, we also have to acknowledge that past performance is all we've got.

The key question is, how much past performance are we looking at?

The longer the timeline, the more information we have. And the more information we have, the better our decisions are likely to be.

By the same token, the less information we have, the worse our decisions are likely to be. So, for instance, in the case of that investment return of 28 percent that was just mentioned, we don't have a lot of data to work with. And if the person secured a verifiable 28 percent return over a time span of three months, it's worth noting that finding that kind of investment is a lot like picking the winner of the Kentucky Derby. It's wonderful when it happens…but it's not the kind of event you want to build a long-term strategy around. And by the way, the same truth holds for an investment that suddenly loses a lot of value in a really dramatic way. Do you sell it, or do you hold on to it? If we want to come up with a responsible answer to that question, we want to look at the longest timeline we can and get the most data we can track down.

Here is the challenge. Most people look at six-month windows of time. And realistically, that's just not enough information for me to make a good recommendation for you. So, I like to look at a much longer time frame.

Fortunately, a gentleman by the name of Dr. Jeremy Siegel (Russell E. Palmer Professor of Finance, the Wharton School, University of Pennsylvania) in his book *Stocks for the Long Run*, has done that research for us. Siegel has tracked the performance of different types of investments, not just over spans of months, or years, or even decades. He has tracked the performance of these investment types over a period of centuries.

Specifically, he's closely monitored the performance of (among other types of investments) both bonds and equities (stocks) since the year 1802, and then annualized them and adjusted them for inflation. That's two centuries and counting—certainly the longest time span I'm aware of. Would you like to hear what he learned?

(The client will almost certainly say "yes" here.)

Siegel determined that equities, over time, are easily the best performing investment. Specifically, he determined that stocks have, over that extraordinary two-centuries-plus time span, delivered a 6.6 percent inflation-adjusted return. But there's a catch: in order to get the benefit of the investment, we have to hold on to the stock.

By the way, something else that Siegel learned was that over that same two-hundred-years-and-counting time span, "owners" (that is, equities) outperformed "loaners" (bonds) by nearly two to one. Bonds returned an inflation-adjusted 3.6 percent over that same very long time span.[1]

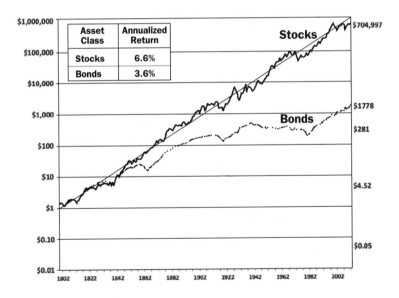

FIGURE 1. Total Real Returns on US Stocks and Bonds, 1802–2012. Adapted from Jeremy Siegel, *Stocks for the Long Run*, 5th ed. (New York: McGraw-Hill, 2014), 6.

So, what can we take away from all this? First, it makes sense to think in the long term, even if you're faced with a sudden loss in value in a given equity investment. Instead of reacting heedlessly and impulsively—which, let's face it, is what a lot of people do when an equity investment suddenly loses a lot of its value—it makes sense to stop, take a deep breath, flick on the high beams, and look down the road a little bit.

Second, it doesn't make sense to expect exaggerated positive returns, like 28 percent, to hold up over realistic time frames.

And third—and perhaps most difficult of all—is the lesson that over the long run, the averages can run in our favor if we pursue a disciplined strategy. Here's the thing about averages: sometimes they are uncomfortable. If you're holding a snowball in one hand and a burning-hot coal in the other, the averages say you're doing fine. But the emotional and physical reality is that you're going through some acute discomfort. Even so…it makes sense to think in the long term. The pain of a sudden rise or drop in the value of a given asset, or in the market as a whole, really does pass over time. Academics call this phenomenon "mean reversion." If we accept Siegel's calculated long-term inflation-adjusted return for equities as 6.6 percent and we experience a 28 percent gain, mean reversion says that future returns will trend down and eventually settle near 6.6 percent. Thus, making structural changes to an investment plan during a market downturn has proven to be unwise historically; it's best to prepare for war in peacetime. By underweighting or overweighting asset classes, good asset allocation models can minimize volatility and help achieve long-term returns. Clients will likely need to be reminded about all the reasons they hold their existing investments when economic forces drive current prices down. They will need to "switch on the high beams" during these periods, and with your help and coaching they will persevere.

KEY TAKEAWAY

Think in the long term. That's when you need the money, after all. Not six months from now, but fifteen, twenty, thirty, or forty years from now!

CHAPTER NINE

TWO STAMPS

Don't judge each day by the harvest you reap
but by the seeds that you plant.
—ROBERT LOUIS STEVENSON

Trust the process. Your time is coming.
Just do the work and the results
will handle themselves.
—TONY GASKINS

THIS COMMUNICATION HACK ILLUSTRATES, in a compelling way, the destructive forces of inflation. The way that many advisors handle the explanation of inflation risk is by putting a chart or graph in front of a client, an approach to which I hope you know by now I am viscerally opposed (with a notable exception). That chart will show the inflation rate as well as how much the value of a dollar degrades over a period of time. I don't know how well most people relate to that kind of display. It seems to me it's guaranteed to get their eyes to glaze over.

But do you know what people do relate to, instantly and immediately? Things that they use every day. That is why when I want to land this point, I will pull out a piece of paper with images of two stamps affixed to it. One is from fifty years ago. The other is from the present day. That's all that shows up on this little piece of paper. Two stamps.

That fifty-year time span between the two stamps is significant because if you're talking to someone in their twenties or thirties who wants to have retirement income to live on in their seventies or eighties, five decades is an emotionally relevant period to look at. You can show your client any fifty-year period you like. I enjoy using 1969–2019. So, what was the big event of that first year? The Apollo 11 moon landing, of course.

FIGURE 2. First Man on the Moon Postage Stamp, US Postal Service, 1969.

Millions of these stamps were issued in 1969 to commemorate the successful effort to put a man on the surface of the moon and bring him home again safely. How much did this first-class stamp cost? Ten cents.

Today, if you want to buy a first-class stamp, the stamp itself won't tell you how much it costs. They just put the word FOREVER on the stamp. That way, they don't have to deal with stamps with the wrong amount printed on them when they raise the price…which happens very often indeed. Currently, a first-class FOREVER stamp costs, not a dime, but fifty-eight cents, and it is likely headed higher. This amounts to around a 4.5 percent postage inflation rate, which is slightly ahead of the Consumer Price Index (CPI) for the same period (~3.9 percent). Here's a current stamp that commemorates the same event, the 1969 moon landing.

FIGURE 3. First Moon Landing Forever Stamp, US Postal Service, 2019.

Now, suppose that instead of showing your prospect that complicated chart that proves how serious the threat of inflation is, you were to show them these two stamps, side by side, on that little piece of paper. And suppose you were to use this powerful visual example to discuss the difference in pricing between the two stamps, and suppose you were to use that discussion to bring home the reality that the purchasing power of our currency does not stand still over time. Then suppose you were to say, "Here's the big question—what do you think a first-class stamp is going to cost in 2069?" (Or whatever year it is that you want to focus on. I like to use the first year the client expects to retire.)

The light bulb goes on. Now the client gets how important this is.

It's at this point that you can start talking numbers. You might choose to say something like the following: "I showed you these stamps for a reason. If you're planning to retire by (year) [or whatever the goal is], we are going to have to set up a strategy that allows you to keep up with these changes in the value of our money. If you don't, then you will have less and less and less money to work with over time. If you put the money in a savings account (in effect, a loan to a bank), you'll earn xx percent, but that likely won't keep up with inflation over time. If you put the money into bonds or CDs, you likely won't keep up either. They historically pay less than 3 percent annually, and the Consumer Price Index over time typically goes up by over 4 percent a year. To make sure your purchasing power remains strong over time, you need something that has been proven to outperform those investments over the long haul."

This transitions nicely into a reinforcement of the importance of investing in equities (see chapter 8).

KEY TAKEAWAY

This particular communication hack is an important one to share with clients who have convinced themselves that bonds and CDs are "safe" investment vehicles. They are not safe from the ravages of inflation, and they won't deliver the 6- to 7-percent-a-year return that investors need to stay ahead of the historically corrosive force of inflation—a return that Siegel's study says is available long-term through equities.

CHAPTER TEN

FOOL'S GOLD

*Money is a terrible master but
an excellent servant.*
—P. T. BARNUM

*Investing should be more like watching
paint dry or watching grass grow. If you want
excitement, take $800 and go to Las Vegas.*
—PAUL SAMUELSON

IT'S POSSIBLE THAT YOUR very early discussions with a new client will involve some beloved preconceived investment idea of dubious long-term potential. A common fixation—one that some clients lose all perspective over—is the possibility of investing in precious metals, notably gold and silver. This communication hack will help with that situation.

As you are no doubt aware, a number of sophisticated marketing campaigns have been waged over the years, and these have had the effect of convincing many people that the precious metals market is the best place to put all of one's hard-earned investment funds. It is not.

The best communication hack you can use here is the simple one of sharing, as many times as necessary, Siegel's remarkable graph. Of course, there is no way to predict with total accuracy the future performance of any investment. That said, however, the past performance of investments *is* the best available indicator of what the future performance trend for any one general category is likely to look like. The longer the history timeline, the clearer the picture. And the picture for gold, in comparison with equities, is a stark one. Take a look:

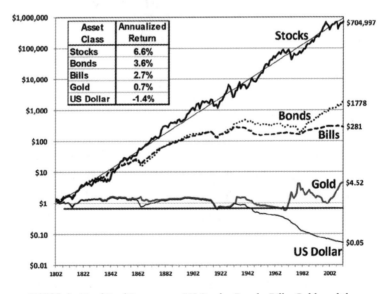

FIGURE 4. Total Real Returns on US Stocks, Bonds, Bills, Gold, and the Dollar, 1802–2012. Jeremy Siegel, *Stocks for the Long Run,* 5th ed. (New York: McGraw-Hill, 2014), 6.

Remind your client once again that they are investing for the long term, not for a three-month or six-month timeline. With this important goal in mind, we can see that the long-term trend could not be clearer. Based on *two centuries' worth of data*, Siegel has clearly demonstrated that putting one's money only in gold tends to deliver a barely measurable positive return over the long term. Yes, there have been major fluctuations, and there have been a lot of entertaining ups and downs; but the reality most relevant to serious investors is the minuscule long-term return (0.7 percent) in comparison to stocks (6.6 percent).

Bonds? They had a return of 3.6 percent in the study. That means you're losing roughly 0.50 percent a year in purchasing power to inflation. (Remember the postage stamp example in chapter 9?)

Just remember that those glossy marketing campaigns, many of which trumpet seemingly extraordinary returns, are all based on short-term windows. Their implied promises are all smoke and mirrors...or in the language made famous during the California gold rush of 1849, fool's gold. Again, Siegel's analysis gives us the longest possible history to look at and is therefore arguably the benchmark for the most conservative approach in terms of setting return expectations that will be reasonable over time.

If we make the mistake of quoting some smaller stretch of time, and/or a narrower data set (say, the performance of gold over the last six months, or the performance of the Dow Jones Industrial Average since World War II), we may be setting unrealistic expectations based on the performance of atypical investments during that period, and we may create problems for ourselves and for our clients down the road. Frame things in a conservative light: focus on the highest possible number of data points over the longest possible period of time. When current returns exceed what happened in that data set, you'll be a hero. I cannot emphasize how important it is to set this reasonable expectation and to coach your client about all the higher numbers they may hear being thrown around by others, usually out-of-context and with very limited data points to verify.

With regard to precious metals, there is a saying: gold is for jewelry. This is not to say there is no place for gold and silver in a well-designed portfolio. A natural resources fund may make sense when it accounts for, say, 5 percent of an investor's exposure. But plowing the majority of one's assets into precious metals, which is what a lot of people are persuaded to do by means of sophisticated marketing campaigns, would be hard to justify long term. Issues of security, verification, and comparatively lax regulation inevitably come into play, as does the very real problem of precious metals like gold and silver not paying dividends, as stocks and bonds do. Natural resources funds typically include investments in companies that mine and extract materials like gold and silver, but also oil, natural gas, platinum, titanium, and other mined materials, known as "hard assets." The bonus here is that many publicly traded mining companies pay dividends, the missing component in the direct ownership of metals. Also, these positions can be traded out of, or increased, with a phone or electronic order.

Another common early discussion with inexperienced investors is the one in which you must find a way to separate them from some cherished business idea, a plan to start a new venture that is regarded, with little evidence, as a "sure thing." Note that the U.S. Small Business Administration reports that 90 percent of small businesses fail within the first five years.[2] While it's true that your client may possess the acumen to make a go of it in starting a business, statistically they have a narrow chance of the venture succeeding. There are a few who may succeed; however, their chances are about 5 percent, or one in twenty— not great odds.

Opening a restaurant is a classic ill-advised obsession, and although there are thousands of possible variations, I'll limit myself here to the restaurant example because it's among the most popular and because the dynamic here is essentially the same as in most other hey-I'll-start-a-business schemes. The investor's chain of logic, if you can call it that, typically goes like this:

- **"I love food/cooking."** For "food" or "cooking," you can insert any passion or interest of the investor's.

- **"So-and-so has a great idea for a restaurant."** Or a basketball school. Or a bed and breakfast. By the way, this person could be a well-meaning friend or relative…or it could be an unscrupulous person out to take advantage of the investor. There are, of course, bad actors in every industry.

- **"Why not invest by doing what I love?"** This isn't really logic, but the client may imagine it is. Asking this question is really the same as asking: "Why not make money watching television? Surfing the Internet? Staring at the lawn?" The answer is: Because for all of the enjoyment we may or may not derive from these activities, there is an extremely low likelihood of an acceptable return. Not only that, but "doing what you love" may not actually turn out to be what you love doing for a living! Sometimes things look a lot better from a distance than they actually are. With this in mind, it is worthwhile to ask the client to do a little "reality check" about all the activities that will actually be required to run this business, activities that they may not end up "loving" as much as they now imagine. For instance, suppose the client tells you that he fondly remembers how good his father was at being a landlord and that he "loves" the idea of following in his father's footsteps. Will he really "love" getting a call about a blocked toilet at one o'clock in the morning? Arranging for lawn-mowing, painting, repairs, and other property maintenance activities that can't, or at least shouldn't, be overlooked? Calling up tenants who fall behind on their rent? Discovering that a tenant skipped out on you while owing some rent, and then discovering that they trashed the unit as well? Help your client call time-out for a moment and consider all the ways in which he or she may simply be buying themselves a job they won't end up liking very much. Their time is valuable. Is this "investment" really the best possible use of that precious resource, time? More to the point, is the financial return on this investment really worth the effort, compared to other things the money could be doing?

For the vast majority of clients with whom you will be working—that is to say, for those who are not experienced venture capitalists (or master chefs) with a clear track record of picking winners—investing hard-earned cash in a restaurant, a shop, or any number of other business ventures is likely to be a strategic mistake. You can land this point powerfully by sharing the story of Muhammad Ali, the self-proclaimed greatest boxer of all time (*TieBreaker.com* has him at number two, behind Sugar Ray Robinson, who had 108 knockouts versus Ali's 37), and one of the most prominent cultural figures of the second half of the twentieth century.[3]

It's possible that your client believes he already knows the story of Muhammad Ali, but it's likely that he doesn't know that the great boxer had a big investment idea that he couldn't let go of: opening restaurants. Twice, Ali signed on with food-service start-ups designed to capitalize on his name and fame. Twice he failed. Both ventures lost serious money. This was part of a larger pattern of poorly considered investments in a wide variety of business opportunities, each based on something Ali "loved."

The untold story is that the Champ was consistently manipulated, and often misled and cheated, by those in his inner circle who urged these schemes on him. (This is one of the reasons he kept fighting past his prime: to make up for his heavy business losses.) If one of the most prominent men on earth could consistently lose money in such undertakings, trying and failing to compete with industry giants, does it really make sense for your client to ignore this risk?

For most people with whom you will be working, the best argument against starting a business as an investment strategy is the simple issue of liquidity. How quickly can you turn a given investment into cash if the need arises? With most equities, the answer is "more or less instantly," because of our regulated exchanges for trading. With a business, the answer is typically either "with great difficulty, after great delay, and with a significant loss" or "never." A willing, qualified buyer must be found.

Here is the reality: all ventures are intended to make profits, but most fail to do so, often through no fault of the entrepreneur. Even with the best idea, the best strategy, and the best possible advice (none of which is a given), market shifts, government regulation, and technological advances can render a new business—and yes, even an entire industry—irrelevant and moribund in a matter of weeks.

The "I'll open a business" fixation is, in the final analysis, another variation on fool's gold. So how do you land that point with your client? Patience and tact inevitably come into play here; but ultimately, in order to help this person benefit from your expertise and guidance, you must look for ways to calmly and diplomatically return the conversation, as many times as possible, to a single, simple question: Is the goal to create a solid financial plan over time...or is it to open a restaurant? (Or a basketball school, a bed and breakfast, or whatever.) If it's the former, you can help. If it's the latter, you can't. You are not a business coach. You are a financial advisor. It's really that simple.

KEY TAKEAWAY

"I'll open a business" is not an investment strategy.

A brief sidenote is in order here. You will, from time to time, find yourself in a situation where someone insists on pursuing an entrepreneurial path, or has already succeeded for many years in doing so. A good reality check with such a client is to have the "five different outcomes" discussion pioneered by the late John F. Savage, an icon of the financial services industry. Savage would sit down with a client who owned, or was about to own, a company, and he would point out that there are five and only five ways to get out of a business: death, disability, retirement, voluntary sale, or bankruptcy. "Of those five options," Savage would ask, "which would you say you prefer most?" This way of approaching the issue had a way of capturing the attention of the business owner. It also leads seamlessly into important discussions about retirement savings, succession planning, key man insurance, disability income coverage, and other important topics that hard-charging entrepreneurs have a way of overlooking. You may want to follow Savage's example, laying out those five possibilities for your client, and see where the discussion leads.

CHAPTER ELEVEN

TULIPS AND BASEBALL

*The individual investor should act consistently
as an investor and not as a speculator.*

—BEN GRAHAM

*The four most dangerous words in
investing are: "this time it's different."*

—SIR JOHN TEMPLETON

THIS COMMUNICATION HACK is helpful when you encounter a prospective client who is following a popular trend in the marketplace and is heavily emotionally invested in the belief that he or she can "make a killing" by investing in a certain stock or sector.

Have you ever heard of "tulip mania"? This was a fascinating market phenomenon that happened during the Dutch Golden Age, back in the 1600s, when ownership of the rarest and most coveted tulip bulbs became highly fashionable in Amsterdam, and some investors, driven by waves of emotion, made absurdly disproportionate investments in specific flowers. Contract prices for certain tulips soared. There are mind-boggling, but apparently accurate, stories of people trading entire estates for a single flower. In February of 1637, the "bulb" burst, and many investors were saddled with heavy losses. This was, apparently, the first recorded example of a speculative bubble in the history of human economics. Everyone got very excited and drove the price of a certain asset up to inconceivable levels—but eventually the market collapsed.

This example of what happened in the Netherlands back then is one that's often cited in economics textbooks, and truth be told, it may be repeated a little too often. So why do I include it here? Because the lesson people derive from this story is usually incomplete.

The lesson we are usually asked to draw from this example in history is that asset prices can sometimes deviate drastically from their intrinsic values and investors need to be aware of this. That's certainly true. It's important to remember that there are cycles of emotion in any market, cycles that result in values that may not correspond with reality. Sometimes the "tulip bulbs" are priced too high. By the same token, sometimes they are priced too low. (We'll be looking at this question of valuation in a little more depth in a later communication hack, one involving cans of tuna fish. Stay tuned.)

However, it's just as important to understand a far more common mistake made by those same investors. They were trying to take advantage of the market's emotional swings by securing huge windfalls with a single investment. In other words, they were trying to make a killing. And this is where our story about tulips actually becomes a story about baseball.

What wins baseball games? Base hits. They're not as exciting as home runs. They may not show up on television as often as home runs do. They don't create the same excitement in the stands that home runs do. But when you get to the end of the season and you look at which teams fail and which ones succeed, what you usually find is that the teams that make the playoffs are the ones that do the best job of getting individual base runners on base.

Sometimes prospective clients want to swing for the fences. They want to do what those "investors" (speculators) back in Amsterdam were trying to do. They get excited about some marketplace trend they have read or seen an online video about—tulips, diamonds, tech, whatever—and they want to win the game with a single dramatic home run. They get fixated on the image of the ball soaring over the fence and the crowd going wild, and they forget about the rest of the game. That's a fantasy, not a strategy. That's not how most teams win the World Series.

As professionals, we have an obligation to call a time-out and remind our clients of the importance of putting together a winning *season* based on sound execution of the fundamentals. To continue the baseball analogy, that means stringing together a lot of bases on balls and base hits. One company, one sector, one commodity is not going to win us the World Series. Setting up a balanced, disciplined offense, one based on consistently putting a lot of runners on base, is what will lead to victory.

The big lesson from Amsterdam, circa 1650, is pretty clear: don't expect a single transaction to set you up for life. By the inch is truly a cinch, by the yard is hard, and by the mile... a trial! Unremarkable small acts consistently applied over time can produce extraordinary results; this is how most will win this game.

―――――――――――

KEY TAKEAWAY

Don't expect a single transaction to set you up for life.

―――――――――――

CHAPTER TWELVE

BY THE INCH, IT'S A CINCH!

A goal without a plan is just a wish.
—ANTOINE DE SAINT-EXUPÉRY

By the inch, it's a cinch!
—RICHARD DOBSON

Time and compound interest can do tremendous things for our clients. But if they forfeit the time component of that, then they'll never catch up. This next communication hack illustrates that point powerfully.

TO DELIVER THIS COMMUNICATION hack to a client, you will need a hinged wooden carpenter's ruler. The length is not important, as long as it has five folding sections. Each section represents one-fifth or 20 percent of our client's working life, or about eight years in a typical forty-year career, spanning from age twenty-five to age sixty-five.

Pull out the ruler and unfold it all the way. Explain to your client that the ruler represents their work lifeline, when extended completely.

For most of us, the capacity for work and income generation diminishes as we get older. If we want to have income to live on in our retirement years, we have to put our money to work generating interest and returns long before that. The earlier we start, the better off we are going to be. Logically, it's the first contributions into a program that are typically worth the most on the day your client retires; put that first contribution off and their retirement may have to wait.

Point out that most people find reasons to put off saving for the future during the first "section" of their working lives. Typically, they may have student loans to pay off, young families to provide for, and a lot of competition for discretionary spending. The convenient time to save comes to no one. Most people don't start their first "real" job and say to themselves, "I need to put away $50 for retirement this week." (FOLD the first section of the carpenter's ruler inward, so that it is now shorter, and say, "They put it off.")

That is typically what happens in our twenties and early thirties. We lose the whole first section when our money could have been earning interest or investment returns for us.

What happens in the next section? Maybe we're buying or improving a first or second home or expanding or starting a family or business. Those are pretty big commitments. Again, we decide it's not a convenient time. We have a lot of responsibilities and a lot of things on our plate. All too often, we lose another section when our money should have been earning returns and interest for us. And with every day we lose, we are missing out on the power of compound interest. (FOLD the first two sections of the carpenter's ruler inward, so that it is now two sections shorter than when you started.)

It's not until later in life that people start thinking seriously about saving for retirement—when they've already lost out on much of their capacity to generate returns. They put themselves at a major disadvantage. And by the way...who wants to retire early? (FOLD the next-to-last section in.) Many of the people with whom we talk tell us their goal is to retire at age fifty-five or even sooner! Very early retirement leaves even less time. (FOLD the last section of the carpenter's ruler inward, so that it is now completely folded up.)

This is where we point out that if we wait until there is a convenient time to save, we will never put ourselves at an advantage.

Once the ruler is all folded up, we need to point out that clients have two choices: they can *work longer* (UNFOLD AND EXTEND the sections on your left)…or they can *start sooner* (UNFOLD AND EXTEND the sections on your right). If clients begin contributions to their retirement plan later on, they must work longer. Starting those critical contributions early opens up the option of early retirement. Start early, retire early. Start later, retire later.

Here is the thing about starting early: it's not the amount that is being contributed that is important; rather, it's the habit that is being established that is all important (not unlike the habits we establish in our business: making calls, scheduling appointments, etc.). Clients who can establish the early habit of saving and investing regularly will have put into place a powerful force that will pay off for them today, through reduced taxable income by contributing to a pre-tax retirement plan, and in the future by creating an income source for early retirement that may be needed to pay for health insurance premiums and to provide for income during the "blackout period" prior to any government pension benefits being payable.

Then we ask the powerful question: *Who can start sooner than today?*

KEY TAKEAWAY

The sooner we start planning and investing, the smaller the steps we need to take consistently to reach our financial goal. By the inch, it really is a cinch!

CHAPTER THIRTEEN

CROP LESSONS

Diversify. In stocks and bonds, as in much else, there is safety in numbers.

—SIR JOHN TEMPLETON

The stock market is a device for transferring money from the impatient to the patient.

—WARREN BUFFETT

ONCE YOU'VE SHARED the carpenter's ruler communication hack and perhaps gained some traction with the idea that the very best day to start generating returns is *today*, you may be tempted to start talking in-depth about diversification and modern portfolio theory. Before you do that and start causing your clients to feel like they've wandered into a college lecture on finance, consider sharing the following communication hack, which will help you land the critical point that diversification is essential.

It's tempting sometimes to think that we want to focus on a single type of investment. Maybe we want one that's really safe.

Maybe we want one that's really adventurous. Maybe there's a specific company in which we're interested. Whatever our predisposition, we can sometimes lose sight of everything else. That's a mistake—not just from an investment standpoint, but from an agricultural standpoint. To understand why this approach isn't such a great idea in the world of finance, let's look at why it isn't such a great idea in the world of agriculture.

If we're in the Midwest region of the United States and we're talking to farmers or even people in businesses that depend on farmers, we can think of this in terms of how farmers choose to plant crops. What is the best strategic choice to make if you have four hundred acres to plant?

Well, for one thing, you don't plant all one crop. You might choose to plant corn and soybeans this year and then switch those out next year, planting corn where last year you had soybeans, and vice versa. That's basic crop rotation. It keeps the soil healthy, and it also has the advantage of limiting your risk. If for some reason there's a problem with one crop, you've still got the other crop to fall back on.

But even after you've made that decision, there's another strategic decision waiting for you. Talk to enough farmers about this, and what you find out is that even when they've allocated two hundred of their four hundred acres to the crop of soybeans, they still find a way to minimize their risk. How do they do that? By using different kinds of seeds for the same crop. You never plant two hundred acres using the same type of seed! You use three or four different strains, each with its own genetic history and makeup, each with subtle advantages and disadvantages.

Why go to the trouble of using different seed types for different corners of your acreage? Because if there's a problem—big or small—that affects one of your seeds, that problem is less likely to adversely affect your entire crop yield. To put it bluntly: Varying your crops, and varying your seed choice within those crops, makes it far less likely that you will experience catastrophic crop failure.

Precisely the same principle holds true in the world of investing. According to *Investopedia*:

> *Modern portfolio theory (MPT) is a theory on how risk-averse investors can construct portfolios to optimize or maximize expected return based on a given level of market risk, emphasizing that risk is an inherent part of higher reward. According to the theory, it's possible to construct an "efficient frontier" of optimal portfolios offering the maximum possible expected return for a given level of*

> *risk. This theory was pioneered by Harry Markowitz in his paper "Portfolio Selection," published in 1952 by the* Journal of Finance. *He was later awarded a Nobel Prize for developing the MPT.*[4]

That's a bit of a mouthful, of course, and not everyone will be receptive to it. But you can get the same basic idea across to your clients by sharing the crop example I've put forth here.

There is some compelling folk wisdom that complements what we are saying here—the old adage never to put all your eggs in one basket. It's interesting to me that this adage has stayed with us even into the twenty-first century, when most of us have no chickens, no eggs to collect, and no baskets to put the eggs into. Yet the advice remains current and sound. If you place all your eggs in one basket and that basket gets dropped by mistake, you're going to have a big problem—the loss of all those eggs. Similarly, if you place all your money in a single volatile commodity—say, sow bellies—and that market collapses for reasons beyond your control or understanding, you've lost your capital. Not a good outcome! (Interestingly, the industrialist, business magnate, and philanthropist Andrew Carnegie had an intriguing spin on this adage: "If you do put all your eggs in one basket, you must watch the basket carefully"—but his billionaire advice isn't really relevant to our clients, because their best course is simply to diversify.)

There is another powerful example you can use to land this point with prospective clients: the idea of the backup plan, the intentional redundancy, the failsafe. Those of us of a certain age still have clear and painful memories of the Challenger disaster of 1986, in which a US space shuttle broke apart just seventy-three seconds into its flight, killing all seven crew members: five NASA astronauts, one payload specialist, and a civilian schoolteacher. The exhaustive investigation that followed determined that the tragedy could have been avoided if the launch team had observed, rather than waiving, a simple redundancy requirement involving a component that cost less than a dollar. Because eliminating the backup safety measure seemed simpler at the time, the crew, the nation, and the world suffered a terrible loss.

KEY TAKEAWAY

Think of diversifying the portfolio as being a little like building in redundancy on a space shuttle's design: It's there to provide protection just in case something goes wrong during the mission. It's a little step you can take that prevents potentially catastrophic failure.

CHAPTER FOURTEEN

KETCHUP AND HABANERO SAUCE

Know what you own and know why you own it.
—PETER LYNCH

If you don't play, you can't win.
—JUDITH MCNAUGHT

AT SOME POINT, it will be time for you to talk about asset class risk with your client. This communication hack will help you do that.

Financial planners and other professionals refer to risk by means of the "beta" concept. A beta of 1 simply means that the security or investment has about the same risk as the overall market. A beta of 2 means that there is double the risk of the overall market. A beta of 0.5 means there is half the risk of the overall market.

This all seems fairly straightforward to us, but the reality is that discussions about risk with those who have not been trained in financial planning and financial concepts can't involve the concept of beta. Unless you're talking with someone who is an engineer or who majored in economics in college, the idea of the beta causes people to disengage. So, what else can we use to get the idea across?

One of my favorite ways to do this is to pull out a (small) bottle of ketchup and a bottle of habanero pepper sauce and place both on the desk in front of me. The use of such physical props has a marvelous way of opening people's minds and securing their attention. So, I strongly recommend that you invest the time to track down these two simple props and keep them in your office or briefcase at all times.

Once these two items are on the table, I will say something like the following:

Investments are a lot like these two condiments. Most people can use ketchup, and lots of it, on almost anything and have no digestive issues at all. But the same is not true for habanero pepper sauce. If you put the same amount of habanero pepper sauce on your hamburger as you would the amount of ketchup that you would use, you would probably find yourself with major stomach problems, or at the very least, an unquenchable thirst.

The same principles apply to our investments. Some are mild. You can enjoy a whole bunch of them without experiencing any trouble. That's one category of investment. I call it the ketchup category. These are investments that are on the safer side, blue-chip (large company) stocks, for instance, or quality bonds. They are not likely to go under, but by the same token, they're not likely to double their return overnight. Although neither can guarantee future values, history has shown this group to be the least volatile.

Another category is more like habanero pepper sauce. These investments likely have much more volatility. You just don't need near as many of them. A little bit goes a long way. That's not to say habanero pepper sauce is somehow bad or wrong. We actually need it to complete the flavor spectrum. But we want to keep it in perspective, and we don't want to overuse it. Habanero sauce investments include things like emerging markets, international markets, cyber currencies, super-small companies, commodities, and metals. Included here are investments that typically and intentionally avoid diversification (sectors) and are given to move up and down in value with rapidity. It's true that these investments may double overnight…but it's also true that they can go out of business unexpectedly. Put simply, the volatility is higher. For most people, these higher-risk categories are neither necessary nor comfortable as the foundation of a portfolio.

This illustration, when accompanied by the physical props that I've mentioned, is incredibly powerful. It also has a long-lasting effect that you can and should take full advantage of. The next time one of your clients calls you up with some risky investment scheme they heard about, you can just say, "Hmmm…habanero sauce," and you will get the idea across. You won't have to start your dialogue over from scratch about the whole concept of risk and volatility.

KEY TAKEAWAY

When it comes to risky, volatile investments, a little bit goes a long way. You don't want your entire portfolio built around them.

CHAPTER FIFTEEN

THE TUNA FISH PRINCIPLE

Courage is being scared to death
but saddling up anyway.
—JOHN WAYNE

The best way to measure your investing
success is not by whether you're beating the
market but by whether you've put in place
a financial plan and a behavioral discipline
that are likely to get you where you want to go.
—BENJAMIN GRAHAM

THIS COMMUNICATION HACK is adapted from a popular presentation delivered by Nick Murray, to whom I am indebted for the example. I use it regularly with my own clients because it's quite powerful visually and because it illustrates, in a compelling and impossible-to-forget way, the importance of keeping market volatility in perspective.

To deliver this particular communication hack, you need to keep an unopened can of tuna fish in your office desk drawer. When the teaching moment about market volatility arises—and I suspect you will know when it does—all you need to do is pull out that can of tuna fish and show it to your prospect or client. He or she will probably be a little surprised to see you pulling out a common grocery store item during a meeting about financial matters. That's fine.

Smile, point to the can, and say, "This is a can of tuna fish. It costs about $1.50 at your local supermarket. Some supermarkets may charge a little bit more, some may charge a little bit less, but that's about the average. Is that about right?"

It's important to ask that question because you want to engage them in the discussion. Remember what we said earlier in the book about participant-centered learning. If it's part of a conversation, the point you are sharing is far more likely to stick.

Virtually every time you ask the question, "Wouldn't you agree?" the person will nod in agreement and say something like, "Yes, that's about what it costs."

Now you say, "Suppose you were to go into the store tomorrow morning and you were to see that there's a big sign next to the tuna fish display, a sign that says, 'Tuna fish, $8 a can.' As a consumer, how do you respond to that?"

Again, you're asking them a question and engaging them in the conversation. Usually, they will tell you that just the other day, they paid $1.50 a can for the same brand of tuna fish, so $8 seems a little excessive. Virtually everyone will give you some variation on "I wouldn't buy it."

At this point, you might say, "So now instead of tuna casserole for dinner tonight, you're probably thinking about buying some chicken, right?" This will certainly get a chuckle.

Say, "But let's say you went into the same supermarket a week later and you saw the same display of tuna fish, only this time there was a sign in front of the cans that said, 'Tuna fish, 5 cans for $1.' Now what would you do?"

Most people will tell you that they would check the date and buy as many cans as they could carry. Assuming it's the same brand that they usually use and that the fish hasn't gone past its expiration date, they are going to stock up on tuna fish.

At this point in the conversation, you might gesture to the can of tuna fish in your hand and say, "By the way, you don't want to use this one. It's been living in my office here for a couple of years."

Right after they laugh at that—and they will—hold up the stock prices page of *The Wall Street Journal*. Point to it. Then say, "My friend, I will tell you a secret. It's all tuna fish. Sometimes, in the world of equity investments, we feel really good about $8 a can, but we won't touch something when it's five cans for $1. How much sense does that make? When the price of tuna drops to five cans for a dollar, maybe that's when we should start thinking about stocking up."

Now you've built in another layer of protection for yourself when your client gets weak knees after news reports of some big swings in the stock market. When that person calls in and says, "Gee, the market is in trouble; the sky is falling. What should we do?" you can just say, "Remember what I told you about tuna fish?"

The client will say, "Oh yes, that's right. I should be buying, shouldn't I?"

And you can then say, "When can you come in?"

(By the way, you don't have to keep a can of tuna in your desk drawer. You can keep it right on your desk. That's what I do. Often, a client will ask if they are interrupting lunch. That's a great invitation to tell the tuna fish story.)

KEY TAKEAWAY

Keep market volatility in perspective.

CHAPTER SIXTEEN

THE YO-YO AND THE STAIRCASE

*The greatest enemy of knowledge is not
ignorance, it is the illusion of knowledge.*

—STEPHEN HAWKING

*The two most powerful warriors
are patience and time.*

—LEO TOLSTOY

THIS IS ONE OF the most popular communication hacks in my arsenal. I always get lots of positive feedback about it. To deliver it, all you need is a pad of paper and a pen.

I begin by saying, "Market volatility and the long-term market average are two different issues. Here's one good way to visualize just how different they are. Picture yourself playing with a yo-yo. What two directions does a yo-yo go in when you're playing with it?"

Naturally, the client will say, "Up and down."

I then say, "Exactly. Up and down." At this point, I draw a simple picture of a yo-yo going up and down. (Better yet, get a yo-yo to keep on hand for this story.) It could look something like this:

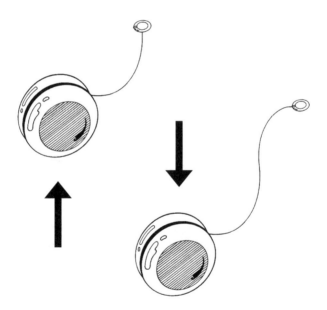

Then say, "So now we know how a yo-yo works. We've got that covered. Now, let me ask you a question. Can you picture yourself playing with the same yo-yo…while you're walking up a set of stairs?"

The client will say, "Sure."

Next, draw a simple staircase on your pad of paper.

Continue by saying, "Now, the daily fluctuations that the media always focuses on—'the market went down,' 'there's a recession on the way,' 'this industry is doing badly,' 'that industry is doing badly'—all of that stuff is the yo-yo. It's never going away. There are going to be ups, and there are going to be downs. It's just in the nature of the way that yo-yos work. They don't stand still. Like equity markets, they go up and down."

Now, put "up" and "down" arrows on the stairs of your staircase.

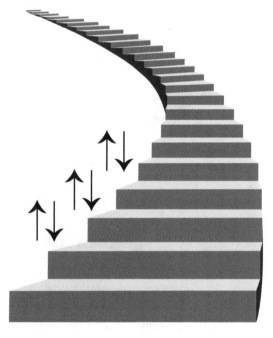

Now say, "The thing is, those short-term fluctuations seem like a big deal, until you realize that the staircase you're walking up—which is the long-term performance of the market—is steadily getting higher and higher. So yes, there are shifts up and down…but the overall trend of the market over the long term is pretty clear. Does this make sense?"

(Remember Siegel and his long-term stock return study? It showed that a diversified portfolio of common stocks in North

America rose at a 6.6 percent average since 1802.[5] Were there daily fluctuations along the way? Absolutely. Should they scare us away from long-term results? Absolutely not!)

The client will nod and say something like, "Yes, I see what you mean."

At that point (being an experienced person) I say, "When I first got into this business in the early 1980s, the Dow Jones Industrial Average had broken one thousand, and it was a really big deal. What's the Dow at now? Do you know?"

The client will give his best guess on the current level of the DJIA.

Then I say, "That's the staircase for you! On any given day, the yo-yo may be up, or the yo-yo may be down…but the long-term direction is a little more important."

Now the client has the mental image of himself or herself walking up that staircase, playing with a yo-yo that goes up and down. He or she gets the message. The short term is the yo-yo, and that's going to go all over the place. But over the long term, we go in one direction.

At this point, I like to throw in a powerful quote from President Franklin D. Roosevelt's fourth and final inaugural address in early 1945. In that speech, FDR summoned the nation to greatness during the waning months of World War II by quoting his old headmaster from the Groton School, which Roosevelt had attended. According to Roosevelt, that headmaster, Endicott Peabody, said the following during a commencement address:

> *Things in life will not always run smoothly. Sometimes we will be rising toward the heights—then all will seem to reverse itself and start downward. The great fact to remember is that the trend of civilization itself is forever upward; that a line drawn through the middle of the peaks and the valleys of the centuries always has an upward trend.*[6]

Wise words to live by—in the stock market, and perhaps everywhere else.

The legendary investment expert Peter Lynch was once asked for his secret to success in stocks. His response was as concise as it was memorable: "Don't get scared out of them." What Lynch was really saying in that single, powerful sentence was the same thing this communication hack is saying to your clients. *Keep your perspective. Don't make big decisions based on the day-to-day, hour-by-hour, or minute-by-minute turbulence of the market. Keep looking forward. And keep heading upwards. Remember, the staircase is what we want—try to ignore the yo-yo.*

KEY TAKEAWAY

Market volatility and the long-term market average are two different issues.

CHAPTER SEVENTEEN

BEN FRANKLIN AND THE ART OF SETTING YOURSELF APART FROM THE COMPETITION

You play basketball against yourself...
your opponent is your own potential.
—BOBBY KNIGHT

Taste the relish to be found in competition—
in having to put forth the best within you.
—HENRY KAISER

In this final communication hack, you learn how to inoculate yourself against the competition...today and tomorrow.

I'VE TALKED TO a lot of financial advisors over the years. One common question that comes up is, "How do I make sure my practice stands out from the competition?" This communication hack is designed to help with that, but in order to put it into practice, you must be ready, willing, and able to build your entire relationship with the client on the foundation of a single, powerful word:

Suitability.

I suspect you've already heard a lot about the vital importance of this word any number of times in relation to your work with clients, but I want to emphasize it here as we approach the end of this book, because once you commit to it, I think you will find that it carries within it the seeds of a competitive advantage that you can count on for months, years, and even decades to come.

As financial planners, we must hold this truth to be self-evident: *any and every recommendation we make to a client, or a prospective client, should be suitable to both the conditions and the person.*

This means no one-size-fits-all advice. This means listening. This means taking the time to understand the other person's unique circumstances, challenges, and objectives, discussing the pertinent points from the prospect's point of view, setting our own goals aside for a moment, and then playing back the information we've gathered to make sure that we've got everything right. Once we're certain of what we're looking at—once we have a clear sense of the other person's needs, goals, and objectives—we make a recommendation that is *suitable* to that individual. We make the recommendation we would want to receive if *we* were in that person's situation.

That should be our process. If we follow such a process, we will position ourselves perfectly to overcome just about any competitive challenge.

Here is why this is so. Once we devote the time, effort, attention, and the financial resources necessary to make a truly unbiased recommendation, one that is uniquely suitable to *this* person, at *this* point in his or her life, based on *this* relationship, something remarkable happens. The relationship starts to work in our favor. The relationship can be leveraged as a barrier to our competitors.

Why? Because nine times out of ten, the client will *realize* that we have set aside our interests in order to focus on theirs. And that means the client will understand that something special has happened. There is now a Trusted Advisor in his or her life.

Such a relationship is worth holding on to—and it is our ultimate competitive edge, because it is so very rare in life.

Think about it. Suppose you want to buy a house, and you find yourself talking to a realtor. For whom does that realtor really work? The seller. They're cajoling you, the buyer, and they're acting as though they are helping you make a decision that's in your best interests, but something about their manner lets you know that their most important commitment is to the seller. You're no fool. You know the seller is the one who has a binding, signed agreement in place already with the realtor and is actually going to be paying them. So, if you're a buyer, you have to wonder: *Is that smile and that handshake for me? Or is it something they're doing for their employer, the owner of the house? Who's working for whom?*

These potential conflicts of interest are, to some degree, inevitable in professional life. At some level, our clients know that, and we know it. Our job is to make sure that clients see ample proof, firsthand, that we really are willing and able to set aside our own personal interests and focus like a laser beam on what they need.

And here is where a little sober self-analysis can come in handy. We must be honest with ourselves so we can be trustworthy advisors for our clients.

Years ago, many advisors literally worked for one carrier. You don't see that as often as you used to…but you do see situations where advisors have financial incentive arrangements with XYZ Insurance that lead them to conclude, over and over again, that one company's products are, by definition, the solution to every client problem. They never even look anywhere else.

You and I have to ask ourselves: *Are we doing business like that?*

If the answer is "yes," then we need to consider making a change. It's fine for our competition to play in that space—in fact, that's where we *want* them to play—but that's not how we are going to build a solid relationship with clients over the long term, nor is it how we are going to establish ourselves as a trusted advisor. Recommending XYZ Life for everything under the sun, regardless of the facts on the ground, is not about the client. It's not about suitability. It's about what's familiar and convenient to us. And that's not going to play out well over the long haul.

Fortunately, in the United States, most of our old-line carriers, and what survives of their agency system, have responded to changes in the marketplace and operate a lot differently than previously. They now cater to all kinds of situations where we have a need for a specialty product or a more customized approach in order to fulfill a client's objectives. The major players offer a much wider range of options to choose from than they once did, so the potential is there for us to look at more than just a couple of familiar products. We need to take advantage of that.

To win in the long haul, you and I must aspire to be—and become—trustworthy advisors. That means we must act in our client's best interests. We must not be beholden to any one company, product, or investment group. We must be beholden only to the client. That must be how we do business. Eliminate or minimize any conflict of interest between you and your client. Typically, a conflict exists when an advisor owns stock or has other forms of ownership in a carrier and they recommend a product to solve a client problem from that same carrier. At a minimum, this needs to be disclosed to the client prior to any action being taken.

We really don't want our business to be all about one wonderful "Swiss army knife" product, supposedly adaptable to all situations. That's a mistake we are going to let our competitors make. For our part, we are going to look with an open mind at the available universe of products and options, and we are going to focus on creating a personalized recommendation (or better yet, a personalized *set* of recommendations) suitable to this unique client. Why are we going to do that? Because we know the future lies in the power of the relationship we build, not in the specific product. What matters is the future of the client with whom we are working. We are going to treat the client like the unique person they are, and we are going to develop a suitable recommendation that is tailored to that client.

My father used to tell me, "Never forget that your future is in the person sitting across the table from you." What he meant was that our future doesn't exist in a textbook, or in a title, at a company, or in a product brochure. It exists in the people we are seeing to and looking out for. I've never forgotten that.

We have to keep asking ourselves the questions our clients are silently asking themselves:

Whose side are you on?

And where is the proof for that? That proof of our commitment needs to show up throughout the relationship.

Here, then, is the communication hack that will help you to demonstrate that proof…and at the same time, set up a powerful barrier against your competition.

PROTECT THE RELATIONSHIP

Most of the advisors I know are vulnerable to the unfortunate phenomenon of a rival swooping in and stealing a client they have worked hard to secure and retain. You don't have to be vulnerable. You can protect the relationship you've worked so hard to build up. Here's how.

At some point during a meeting where you are examining an important question of personal financial strategy in an effort to create a suitable recommendation, you're going to follow the time-tested advice of one of the Founding Fathers of the United States, Benjamin Franklin. Franklin famously shared some wise advice for making important decisions. Perhaps you've heard of it. He would draw a line down the middle of a sheet of paper, place the reasons *for* a given course of action on the right-hand side and the reasons *against* that same course of action on the left-hand side. After he had listed all of the possibilities, he would evaluate both lists and make his decision based on which written list had the most compelling and powerful reasons supporting it.

As you evaluate the pros and cons of the decision before you and your client, whatever that decision may happen to be, I want you to use the same technique. I want you to follow Franklin's example and use competing written lists to conduct a thorough and meaningful examination of both the benefits and disadvantages of the proposed course of action—*from the client's point of view.*

Then I want you to make your own best recommendation to the client, based on your own responsible analysis of the factors the two of you have entered into those two columns. In other words, I want you to use the two-column approach to *prove why what you are recommending is uniquely suitable to this client.* It should go without saying that you cannot expect to do this without first engaging in a long period of intelligent questioning, followed by active listening.

Once you have made your best recommendation—and the client has had the chance to see firsthand not only how your mind works, but how closely what you are recommending suits their needs, goals, and objectives, and how committed you are to the process of evaluating a complicated set of options and protecting the client's interests—I want to suggest that you follow some advice that my father gave me years ago.

I want you to tell your client specifically, and in a way that cannot possibly be misunderstood, that you operate in a competitive business.

This is important, because we can't assume that everyone will accept or understand that principle when they walk in our door. A schoolteacher may not think of financial advisors as competing with each other, since they work in an environment where they are not required to compete with other teachers. By the same token, any number of businesspeople may be used to thinking of financial advisors as being roughly similar to accountants or attorneys, professionals who often overlap in the services they provide to the same client. With us it is different. And we need to make that clear.

To land that point, I suggest you say something like this: "Mr./ Ms. Client, you've now had the chance to see how I work. This relationship means a lot to me. And I hope you can see how seriously I take my responsibility to provide you with the best possible service, the most rigorous analysis, and the soundest advice for your unique situation. I need to say something important to you now. In the weeks or months or years ahead, it's very likely that you're going to receive some kind of pushback from some other financial professional, someone who questions some part of the advice that I'm giving you. Of course, it's up to you whether you take such a call, but if you do decide to take the call, I want you to know that there is going to come a point where another financial professional, motivated by the desire to hold on to a client or acquire a new one, is going to try to undermine the work we've just done…without conducting the same kind of in-depth analysis that you and I have just spent our time on. Instead of looking around all the corners, instead of asking all the right questions and tracking down the relevant answers, as you and I have done today, this person is going to simply *object* to what I recommend…without giving you any meaningful reasons for that objection and without doing any work to determine what is really *suitable* given your unique situation. And when that happens, I want you to know that you are going to be putting yourself in a position where that person is going to be insulting your intelligence and my integrity. So can I just please ask you to be aware of that if you do choose to take that call?"

Of course, the new client will nod and agree to what you have suggested. When the call does come—and you can be certain it will—your client will be more likely to step back and think, *Hang on, this is exactly what I was warned about during that meeting. This person is out to insult my intelligence...and my advisor's integrity.* And if you have executed this communication hack properly, your competitor won't even be able to begin that conversation with your client, because you will have protected the relationship you've worked so hard to create.

KEY TAKEAWAY

Build your relationship with the client on the foundation of the powerful word *suitability.*

EPILOGUE

THE LINCOLN STANDARD

Nice guys may appear to finish last,
but usually they are running in a different race.
—KEN BLANCHARD

I believe that you can get everything in life you
want if you will just help enough other
people get what they want.
—ZIG ZIGLAR

AS WE CLOSE THIS BOOK, I would like to leave you with this thought:

The most successful financial advisors are those who do the right thing by closely attending to their clients' best interests.

It is vitally important that we find ways to maintain a constant focus on those words: *best interests.* I hope the tools I have shared with you in these pages will help you sustain that focus.

My advice to you as we part is simple: do the right thing and let that objective be your guide. That's a moral standing, of course, but I have found that it's also the most powerful competitive advantage there is.

I'll conclude with a true story that's relevant, I think, to what I've shared with you in this book. President Abraham Lincoln was not much of a churchgoer, and he was often hounded by the press about why this was the case. In those days, as in these, the press was out to capture a good headline, and some of the best headlines had to do with whether the president was an agnostic, an atheist, or a follower of some religion other than Christianity. For the longest time, apparently, Lincoln sidestepped these queries, until finally a reporter cornered him and asked him, "What is your religion, Mr. President?"

Lincoln looked him in the eye and said, "When I do good, I feel good. When I do bad, I feel bad. And that's my religion."

That comeback has stuck with me for years. It's a pretty good story. It's a pretty good standard for financial advisors...and, I believe, everyone else. Do good, feel good. If you follow that simple standard, I know you'll be setting yourself and your clients up, not for short-term gain, but for enduring success, the kind of success that makes you feel good in the long run. And that is exactly what I wish for you and your clients: success that lasts. That's the journey I hope you are inspired to make, and I hope the process I have shared with you in this book has made the direction of that journey a little clearer.

I would like to be your companion on that journey. Let's keep in touch! Visit me online at richarddobson.net to learn about resources that support these communication hacks and to share your own experiences in using them.

KEY TAKEAWAY

The most successful financial advisors are those who do the right thing by closely attending to their clients' best interests.

APPENDIX

FIVE THINGS FINANCIAL PLANNERS DO TO MAKE GOOD CONVERSATIONS WITH PROSPECTS IMPOSSIBLE

*The single biggest problem in communication
is the illusion that it has taken place.*
—GEORGE BERNARD SHAW

*Listen with curiosity. Speak with honesty.
Act with integrity. The greatest problem with
communication is we don't listen to understand.
We listen to reply. When we listen with curiosity,
we don't listen with the intent to reply.
We listen for what's behind the words.*
—ROY T. BENNETT

MANY PEOPLE FIND CONVERSATIONS with financial advisors so off-putting that they can't relax around us and don't feel safe enough to share important information with us.

Why is that the case? Because unintentionally, we don't make them feel comfortable in the very early phases of the relationship.

Simply put, too many financial planners make basic mistakes when it comes to establishing commonality with the people they hope to do business with. Typically, they make these mistakes in the very earliest phases of the very first discussion. As a result of our own failure to establish commonality—a failure to put the prospect at ease and make sure he or she knows we're human and approachable and interested in listening—we make our prospects feel uncomfortable from the starting bell. Guess what? People who are uncomfortable don't open up. And people who don't open up to us don't take part in good conversations. And people who don't take part in good conversations don't end up doing business with us.

Consider the following list of five things financial planners typically do that make their prospects tense up instead of relaxing…and the things they *could* be doing to put prospective buyers at ease.

1. Botching the first face-to-face moment. People will form their impression of how this relationship is going to go, and whether it is going to be useful to them, not in hours, not in minutes, but in seconds. If you make the prospect wait for a long time before being ushered into the Inner Sanctum, if you force them to watch the news from the TV mounted in the waiting room (which may be depressing), if you fail to greet them with a firm, friendly handshake, look them in the eye, and say you're glad to meet them and mean it, then the battle for this person's business may be over before it has even begun.

Manage the initial face-to-face experience carefully. Make sure it is positive. And turn off the news in the waiting room. Find a more upbeat, appropriate channel. All too often, the TV is tuned to MSNBC or a financial news network. Think about what that means. You want them to think about the long term and put market "bumps" in perspective...but you've got a talking head on the screen hyperventilating about the latest market problem or worrying about what the next one will be. Is that really how you want to set up your first conversation... or any conversation?

2. Talking about your own credentials. Boasting that you went to a well-known business school, or achieved some professional certification that your competition lacks, may seem like a good way to establish or enhance your credibility, but in reality, it turns people off. They wouldn't be talking to you in the first place if they suspected you didn't have the background required to make good recommendations. Instead of pointing to the diploma on your wall or bragging about your own background, talk about how committed you are to serving the client and helping him or her build a solid financial future. Your commitment to the relationship is far more important to the prospect than your degree or accreditation. In fact, people respond positively to businesses that contribute to their communities. A few office pictures of you and your team volunteering at a community event won't go unnoticed, according to many client feedback studies, and are much better than bragging.

> *The measure of a person is the worth*
> *of the things they care about.*
> —MARCUS AURELIUS

3. Emphasizing your product or the company whose product you represent. Lots of financial planners say things like, "We're in the top 10 percent of Colossus Insurance Company representatives nationwide," or "We specialize in XYZ product from Colossus, which has a great reputation." This kind of thing only turns prospects off. Why? Because the prospective client isn't interested in your loyalty to any insurance company or broker/dealer and suspects that it may get in the way of your loyalty to him or her. And when you mention life insurance policies or annuities at the outset of the conversation, your prospect likely has no idea how to evaluate those products or whether they are relevant to his or her world. Instead of touting your connection to the specific product or company, talk about the *kinds of clients* you have helped in the past and how long you've been helping them. For instance: "We've been helping homeowners and aspiring homeowners in the metropolitan Baltimore area plan for their financial future since 1995." Be known for solving your clients' problems, rather than the products you may recommend.

4. Making the prospect feel like a student and/or throwing lots of technical terminology at him or her. This is a mistake at any point in the relationship, but it's particularly dangerous in the very early going. Your job is not to lecture this person. Are you "talking at" or "talking with"? Your job is to make him or her feel comfortable enough to trust you with the future of his or her family. So, avoid going into the Lecture Mindset, and avoid words and phrases that you know are meaningful primarily to financial professionals. Instead, learn about this person's background, hopes, and aspirations. Look for opportunities to share the communication hack process I've described in this book. Last but not least, *tell stories from your own experience.* Say things like, "You know, I recently had a case where we faced a similar situation. What happened there might be relevant."

5. Not finding some kind of common ground. It is a potentially fatal mistake among financial service professionals to launch into the "business portion" of the meeting without having engaged in any of the meet-and-greet chitchat that allows prospects to determine for themselves that they have some shared interest or acquaintance in common with you. Use the first few moments of the meeting to gently put the focus on the other person and to find out where there are areas of social overlap. For instance, do you know any of the same people? Do your kids go to the same schools? Have you grown up in the same area? Do you follow the same sports teams? I'm not suggesting that you can or should spend a great deal of time on such topics, but for most prospects, it is going to be important that you use the initial "icebreaker" phase of the conversation to establish some kind of common ground. If all else fails, find out where the prospect has vacationed or plans to vacation next—and express suitable admiration for that destination. Once you have found a way to establish person-to-person commonality with the prospective client, you will find that the quality of the communication improves dramatically.

NOTES

1. Jeremy J. Siegel, *Stocks for the Long Run: The Definitive Guide to Financial Market Returns and Long-Term Investment Strategies*, 5th ed. (New York: McGraw-Hill, 2014).

2. Sean Bryant, "How Many Startups Fail and Why?" *Investopedia*, last updated November 9, 2020, https://www.investopedia.com/articles/personal-finance/040915/how-many-startups-fail-and-why.asp.

3. Connor Howe, "The 30 Greatest Boxers of All Time," *TieBreaker.com*, June 18, 2019, https://www.tiebreaker.com/30-greatest-boxers-of-all-time/.

4. Peter Westfall, "Modern Portfolio Theory (MPT)," *Investopedia*, last updated September 10, 2021, https://www.investopedia.com/terms/m/modernportfoliotheory.

5. Siegel, *Stocks for the Long Run*.

6. Franklin D. Roosevelt, "Fourth Inaugural Address," transcript of speech delivered at Washington, DC, January 20, 1945, https://avalon.law.yale.edu/20th_century/froos4.asp.

ABOUT THE AUTHOR

Richard Dobson, Jr., CFP, entered the financial services industry in June of 1980 and attended the University of Northern Iowa, where he earned a BA in Business/Marketing in 1981. Mr. Dobson holds Iowa life and health licenses and is 6, 26, 27, 51, 63, and 65 FINRA series qualified.  He is executive vice president and chief compliance officer of American Financial Securities, a FINRA broker-dealer, and president of American Financial Management, an SEC-registered Investment Adviser firm.

Mr. Dobson is a life member of the Million Dollar Round Table (MDRT), where he has volunteered and served extensively as past divisional vice president; past chair of the MDRT Finance Committee; past president of the MDRT Foundation (2017); main platform chair, Program Development Committee; and he has been a ConneXion Zone, Focus Session, and Main Platform annual meeting speaker. He is a member of the National Association of Insurance and Financial Advisors (NAIFA) since 1984 and has served as board trustee and officer of NAIFA-Iowa and past chair of the NAIFA-National Investment Committee.

Mr. Dobson has given hundreds of continuing education classes, workshops, and keynote addresses and have helped thousands of clients and advisors move toward success over the last forty years. He resides in Cedar Falls, Iowa.

www.richarddobson.net

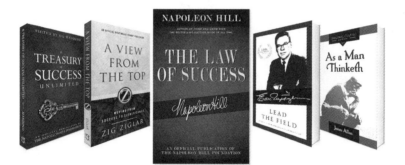